Knowledge Automation

Founded in 1807, John Wiley & Sons is the oldest independent publishing company in the United States. With offices in North America, Europe, Asia, and Australia, Wiley is globally committed to developing and marketing print and electronic products and services for our customers' professional and personal knowledge and understanding.

The Wiley Corporate F&A series provides information, tools, and insights to corporate professionals responsible for issues affecting the profitability of their companies, from accounting and finance to internal controls and performance management.

Knowledge Automation

How to Implement Decision Management in Business Processes

ALAN N. FISH

WILEY

John Wiley & Sons, Inc.

Published by John Wiley & Sons, Inc., Hoboken, New Jersey.
Published simultaneously in Canada.

For general information on our other products and services or for technical support, please contact our Customer Care Department within the United States at (800) 762-2974, outside the United States at (317) 572-3993 or fax (317) 572-4002.

Wiley also publishes its books in a variety of electronic formats. Some content that appears in print may not be available in electronic books. For more information about Wiley products, visit our web site at www.wiley.com.

FICO is a trademark of Fair Isaac Corporation in the United States and other countries.

Library of Congress Cataloging-in-Publication Data:

Fish, Alan N.
  Knowledge automation : how to implement decision management in business processes / Alan N. Fish.
      p. cm. — (Wiley corporate F&A series)
  Includes index.
  ISBN 978-1-118-09476-1 (cloth); ISBN 978-1-118-22351-2 (ebk);
  ISBN 978-1-118-23679-6 (ebk); ISBN 978-1-118-26184-2 (ebk)
  1. Information technology.—2. Decision making.—I. Title.
    HD30.2.F574 2012
    658.4'038011—dc23
                                                    2011042679

Printed in the United States of America

10 9 8 7 6 5 4 3 2 1

*To Alan Turing (1912–1954), on whose shoulders
the giants whose shoulders we stand on, stand.*

Contents

Foreword

FIRST CAME ACROSS Alan's work in 2009 when he introduced me to the concepts at the heart of Decision Requirements Analysis. I was impressed by the approach he outlined and its potential for improving the analysis and design of decision management systems. I have been working in decision management for most of the last decade, spending much of that helping companies use business rules and predictive analytic technology to automate and improve business decisions. Alan's approach to gathering, modeling, and managing decision requirements immediately struck me as the right way to approach this problem. I have been using it with my clients ever since.

Decision management is a well established approach that focuses on automating and improving operational business decisions, including the many micro-decisions that impact a single customer or a single claim. In the years I have been working on decision management systems, the approach has become increasingly well known and adopted. Building decision management systems requires a solid platform for managing decision-making logic—a business rules management system—and the ability to integrate predictive analytic models with this logic. It also requires the ability to effectively identify, model, refine, and manage the requirements for such a system in a decision-centric way.

Take one company I was working with recently. They were struggling, trying to adopt a business rules management system into a process-centric culture. Using Alan's approach, we focused their energy on their decisions, on the dependencies between their decisions, and on the information and knowledge required by their decisions. Successful adoption of the business rules management system and a new appreciation for the role of decisions alongside processes were the result.

Many companies make the mistake of assuming that their existing requirements gathering and management processes will work well as they adopt business rules and a business rules management system. In fact, existing approaches lack the focus on decisions needed for success and offer little or no help in actually analyzing decisions. Similarly, those using predictive analytic models often lack a formal or repeatable approach to defining the decisions their models are meant to assist. This is where Decision Requirements Analysis shows its worth.

This book is very timely. Decision management systems are increasingly topical and the focus of both the business rules and predictive analytics industries is shifting to a conversation about decisions and decision automation. In the past nine years I have helped dozens of companies that are implementing business rules and predictive analytics. I've spoken with literally hundreds more. Decision management systems are a powerful way for companies and organizations to improve their business and create a more agile, more analytic and more adaptive business. To succeed companies need more than great technology, they also need to be able to analyze and design these systems. Alan's work on Decision Requirements Analysis is a critical component of this.

With this book, Alan has written a practical and straightforward guide to using the Decision Requirements Analysis approach. A quick but thorough introduction to knowledge, decision-making, and the role of automated decision services in business processes sets the scene. The core chapter introduces the modeling approach and the workshop that goes with it. Alan shows how the approach helps at every stage of a project, from discovery to implementation, and outlines a great initial set of common decision patterns to help you get started. If you plan to analyze and model decisions—and you should—this book will show you how to do so.

I feel strongly that this is the best approach for modeling decisions out there, which is why I use it with my clients and recommend it in my most recent book.

—James Taylor

James is CEO and Principal Consultant, Decision Management Solutions, and is based in Palo Alto, CA. He is the author of Decision Management Systems: A Practical Guide to Using Business Rules and Predictive Analytics *(IBM Press, 2011). He is an active consultant, working with companies all over the world, and can be reached at james@decisionmanagementsolutions.com.*

Preface

ORGANIZATIONS ARE CONSTANTLY searching for ways to make their business processes more effective, less costly, and more agile. Recently, the strategies adopted increasingly involve three technologies:

1. Decision management: the use of predictive analytics and business rules to optimize and automate decision-making, allowing day-to-day operational strategy to be controlled directly by process managers, rather than IT.
2. Business process management systems (BPMS): systems that allow business processes to be modeled as sequences of activities, and then ensure compliance in those processes by executing the models.
3. Service-oriented architecture (SOA): the provision of software functionality as loosely coupled, reusable services, which encapsulate their internal logic to hide it from the consumers.

This book addresses the intersection of these fields. Using a combination of all three technologies, it is possible to encapsulate business knowledge in services, consumed by the BPMS, which automatically make optimal operational decisions for the organization. This is knowledge automation (see the following graphic).

Process automation projects are always large and complex in any case, and usually represent a substantial strategic investment by the organization. After deploying any new IT infrastructure required, the organization faces the challenges of process redesign and organizational change. If operational decision-making is to be included in the scope of what is to be automated, we have an additional task: creating the services that are to make the decisions. Such "decision services" can be very complex, including sophisticated analytic models, hundreds or thousands of business rules, and elaborate calculations.

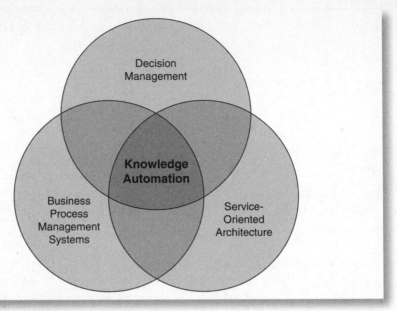

Knowledge Automation

Knowledge automation projects therefore need careful management if they are to be successful. Potential problems include:

- Development projects that deliver late or run significantly over budget
- Facilities that are not accepted by the users because they do not display a sufficient degree of competence
- Systems that are hard to maintain or get more confused year by year

These problems are often due simply to the lack of any clear definition of the requirements for decision making early in the project. In my experience, this is due never to a lack of effort, but rather to using the wrong approach. When these projects fail they have usually gone wrong at the very beginning.

There are a number of excellent books providing theoretical and technical background to decision management, business rules, and predictive analytics, and explaining why they are a good thing (a Suggested Reading list is provided in the back of the book). Although I include some basic background on the technologies and the benefits, this is not the main subject of this book. I assume you are already committed to or involved in a knowledge automation project, or at least have some understanding of the benefits of decision management and are considering the feasibility or planning of such a project. The main purpose of this book is to give you a practical step-by-step guide to how to go about it.

Over the years I have been involved in a great many projects to build decision services for various business domains. Perhaps it is just my natural laziness, but I have developed a way of working that makes projects simpler and reduces the risks of failure and overrun. Simplicity is an underrated virtue: The methods we choose should be those that make tasks easier for people. People find a task easier when it has a clearly defined scope—that is, they know exactly what they have to do—and a clearly defined structure—that is, they can see how it can be broken into smaller tasks.

The method I describe in this book is Decision Requirements Analysis (DRA), which is used to define the scope and structure of the decision-making that is to be automated. DRA is quick and simple to use, but allows a domain of business decision-making to be defined with great clarity, because:

- It ties the decision-making to specific points in the business process: the decision points.
- It is based on a simple diagram of the structure of the decision-making: the Decision Requirements Diagram (DRD).
- It allows the scope of decision-making to be defined by listing the decision points, and drawing boundaries around parts of the DRD.

The primary statement of requirements in DRA is therefore a picture, a common language easily understandable by all involved: the project sponsors, project managers, process experts, business analysts, technical architects, and development team. The DRD allows the requirements for the automation of decision-making to be discussed and agreed by everyone at the start of a project. The structure it reveals then gives shape to the design, the implementation, and the project itself. I hope you will find it useful.

HOW TO READ THIS BOOK

Read it all. Go on, it's not long and not too technical—just read it all. Authors are expected nowadays to provide alternative paths through the text, tailored for different readers, but the approach I suggest depends on the idea that the structure of decision-making revealed in the DRD provides a framework for all the levels of a project, right from top to bottom, so to appreciate the value of the approach you need to see its full gamut. The structure of the book follows these levels:

Chapter 1 introduces the concept of the value of knowledge, first at the macroeconomic level with its contribution to economic growth, then in terms of its specific value to individual organizations. It provides a brief introduction to the principles of decision management, and describes decision yield, a way of measuring the benefits of automating decisions.

Chapter 2 looks at how business processes may be redesigned to automate operational decision-making, through the use of BPMS that call decision services at key points. It suggests ways of rationalizing the business process to derive maximum benefit from decision management, and provides a simple template originations flow as an example.

Chapter 3 provides some background on the most important technologies used for encapsulating business knowledge in decision services: business rules, algorithms, and predictive analytics, and explains when each should be used. It then describes how decision management involves a constant cycle of data through the BPMS, predictive analytics, and the decision services.

Chapter 4 presents the principles of Decision Requirements Analysis and introduces the Decision Requirements Diagram, which represents a domain of decision-making as a network of decisions, knowledge areas, and data areas. It describes in detail how to run a structured workshop resulting in the DRD and all the supporting information required to create an automation scoping document.

Chapter 5 shows how to use the structure of the DRD to scope, estimate, plan, and manage a project to implement a set of decision services, and how the same structure can be used as a basis for the design, development, configuration, and testing of those services, so that all activities are aligned efficiently to support a "knowledge production line," resulting in an implementation with full traceability of all components back to the original requirements.

Chapter 6 provides a set of commonly occurring decision patterns, useful as templates, with simplified partial DRDs and object models. Finally, it suggests a number of alternative ways of handling decision-making where decision services and business users must collaborate on reaching a decision, and suggest situations in which these might be used.

 INTENDED READERSHIP

A knowledge automation project involves the participation of many people in a great cascade of activity. This book is intended to help them all.

- Executives in organizations considering or implementing automated decision-making, especially the CEO, CIO, and CFO, who need to understand the basic principles of the technologies and the issues involved in implementing them
- IT architects involved in the procurement of BPMS, BRMS, and analytic products, who need to know the functionality required for knowledge automation and how the products should interoperate
- Analysts working in the design or redesign of business processes to use automated decision-making, who need an approach that will result in a clean and efficient process design
- Change managers and personnel managers, who need to understand how the roles of staff change when knowledge automation is introduced and how to be involved in defining that change
- Managers responsible for aspects of organizational performance to be addressed by the automation (e.g., product managers, risk managers, and process managers), who need to ensure that the new systems will support them in more agile and effective management
- Project managers, who need to know how a knowledge automation project should be structured and managed so as to minimize costs, timescales, and risks
- IT architects involved in the design of systems to automate decision-making, who need a set of principles for specifying a set of decision services and designing their internal structure and interface signatures
- Analysts responsible for defining the business requirements for automated decision-making, who need a top-down approach for discovering and codifying business knowledge

I hope the book will also be of some interest to those whose concerns are more theoretical than practical.

- Standards bodies and consortia, which are interested in defining executable models of decision-making encompassing multiple forms of business knowledge
- Academic institutions running courses in IT and AI, which wish to provide students with a robust methodology for knowledge automation
- General readers, who are interested in what happens behind the scenes when they apply for a financial product and how institutions make automatic decisions that affect them directly

SCOPE

This is a "how to do it" guide, not a theoretical treatise, intended principally to be used by those actually involved in knowledge automation projects. It must therefore be directed at the prevailing paradigm for process automation: BPMS and SOA. In particular (this will be discussed in detail in Chapter 2), it assumes that stateless decision services will be called from process flows managed by a BPMS. So, for example, it neglects the emerging field of complex event processing (CEP), in which decision-making is triggered by the detection of an event, rather than by a task in a process flow. However, the central concepts in this book—concerning how to represent and implement the structure of automated decision-making—are applicable however that decision-making is triggered.

The book aims to be product-neutral throughout and therefore restricts itself mainly to functional issues, rather than technical ones. You will find here no comparison of the facilities of different BRMS products, no explanation of how inference actually works in a BRMS, and no discussion of the systems architectures required to support BPMS and BRMS. As a result, I hope the methods and techniques I describe in this book will be applicable whichever products and architectures your organization elects to use.

As suggested by the title, the book focuses on the automation of operational decision-making in business processes, rather than any other uses of decision management technologies (e.g., product design and marketing, business intelligence, and data mining). It also uses examples taken from mainstream application areas of process automation (to be frank, those that are most familiar to me). These include originations, account management, and claims management in banking, retail credit, general insurance, life insurance, and health insurance. Of course, knowledge automation can be applied in many other scenarios.

Acknowledgments

I owe a profound debt of thanks to many people:

- My wife Cath for her unswerving support while I worked on this book, and my younger children Oscar and Penny, who have had to tolerate my frequent absences.
- My colleagues at FICO, for indulging me in the implementation of these ideas, helping to promote them in the industry, and being such good company when working on-site.
- All the clients on many projects, from whom I have learned so much, for giving me their trust and hospitality and making this work so thoroughly enjoyable.
- My friend Roger Farmer, for useful advice, a shot of confidence, and too many shots of tequila.
- James Taylor, for his support, his fount of knowledge, and for kindly agreeing to provide the Foreword.
- Paul Konnersman, for engaging in lengthy correspondence on approaches to decision automation, and allowing me to cite his work, even though he doesn't entirely agree with me.
- My late father, for teaching me how to think about systems. I miss arguing with him.

I am sketching this introduction in the brick-arched cellars of Jazzland, the oldest jazz club in Vienna. I'm eating cevapcici; drinking Austrian beer; and watching Vincent Herring on sax, Danny Grisset on piano, Markus Schieferdecker on bass, and Joris Dudli on drums: all astonishing musicians and a seriously cool crew. I must confess, I am extraordinarily privileged to be able to work in an interesting field, doing a job I love, with intelligent clients and colleagues, in beautiful places. Long may it continue.

Knowledge Automation

CHAPTER ONE

The Value of Knowledge

W HAT COMES INTO YOUR HEAD when you hear the word "knowledge"? Dusty books in the libraries of ancient universities, perhaps, or men in white coats with big foreheads? My aim in this first chapter is to change the way you think about knowledge. It is not an abstract concept divorced from the world of business; it is a tangible corporate asset. You can manufacture it, own it, buy and sell it, build it into machines that make profits for you: It is real *stuff* that has *value*. This is a crucial concept in understanding the potential benefits of decision management.

I'm going to start right at the top with a brief discussion of modern macroeconomic theories of knowledge before looking more practically at how organizations can measure and exploit the value of their own business knowledge.

 ## THE ECONOMICS OF KNOWLEDGE

The past 50 years have seen a revolution in our understanding of the drivers of economic growth. Classical economic theory addressed labor, land, and capital. In much the same way, modern economic theory now addresses human knowledge, and its contribution to the growth of economies.

1

Neoclassical Growth Theory

Theories of growth proposed in the 1950s, such as those of Robert Solow[1] and Trevor Swan[2] were based squarely on physical capital: objects such as machinery and stock. These were called "neoclassical growth models." According to neoclassical theory, physical capital is assumed to be subject to the law of diminishing returns: the principle that if you keep increasing any single factor of production, the output you achieve from each unit of input will eventually decrease. This assumption is mathematically convenient, because it results in a model economy that always converges to a unique steady state. In other words, under any constant conditions, growth will slow down and eventually stop.

Figure 1.1 shows the attitude prevailing at the time. Bill Phillips built this hydraulic computer—MONIAC—in 1949, using water flowing around pipes and tanks to simulate the U.K. economy. This was a sophisticated and accurate model, but the message is very clear: the economy finds its own level.

Neoclassical models could not explain long-term growth, and were not intended to. In this approach, long-term growth is accounted for by external influences. Robert Solow introduced technical knowledge as such an "exogenous variable." [3] He assumed that technology was improving steadily without any influence from the economy being modeled; it simply happened, providing the external stimulus that kept the economy growing. Such a model allows you to measure the *effects* of technological progress, or to decide, for example, the optimal savings rate given a certain rate of progress. Because of this, Solow's model became widely used in economic analysis and earned him the 1987 Nobel Prize for Economics. What his model cannot do, however, is help you to determine economic policy to *achieve* technological progress.

New Growth Theory

The thrust of more recent theories of growth has therefore been to "endogenize" knowledge: to bring it within the terms of the model as an internal variable and use it to explain the observed growth of economies. Robert Lucas explains why such models are so important:

> Is there some action a government of India could take that would lead the Indian economy to grow like Indonesia's or Egypt's? If so, *what*, exactly? If not, what is it about the "nature of India" that makes it so? The consequences for human welfare involved in questions like these are simply staggering: Once one starts to think about them, it is hard to think about anything else.

FIGURE 1.1   Bill Phillips with MONIAC

This is what we need a theory of economic development *for*: to provide some kind of framework for organizing facts like these, for judging which represent opportunities and which necessities.[4]

According to Charles Jones and Paul Romer, to account for the most important facts, "a growth model must consider the interaction between ideas, institutions, population, and human capital. Two of the major facts of growth—the extraordinary rise in the extent of the market associated with globalization and the acceleration [in growth rates] over the very long run—are readily understood as reflecting the defining characteristic of ideas, their non-rivalry." [5]

The concept of rivalry is central to understanding the importance of human knowledge in economic growth. Most physical goods are *rival*; only one person can make use of them at a given time. People have to compete for ownership of land, money, or physical goods. Ideas, however, are *non-rival*; people do not have to compete for them. A single idea may be used simultaneously by many people without being depleted in any way; in fact, the opposite applies: the value of the idea is proportional to the number of people using it.

Because of this, non-rival goods are not subject to the law of diminishing returns, as physical goods are; they are actually subject to *increasing* returns. For example, a programming language is a non-rival good. One programmer using the language does not prevent another from using it at the same time. On the contrary, the value to the programmer of using a particular language is increased if many other people use the same language, and the costs of using the language are decreased. It is these scale effects of non-rivalry that cause growth to accelerate, rather than find its own level. As Romer explains in his Stanford University biography:

> I wondered why growth rates had been increasing over time. . . . Existing theory suggested that scarcity combined with population growth should be making things worse, but they kept getting better at ever faster rates. New ideas, in the form of new technologies, had to be the answer. Everyone "knew" that. But why do new technologies keep arriving at faster rates? One key insight is that because ideas are non-rival or sharable, interacting with more people turns out to make us all better off. In this sense, ideas are the exact opposite of scarce objects.[6]

The other important characteristic of goods in economic theory is whether they are *excludable*: whether it is possible to prevent people having access to them unless they have paid. The two dimensions of rivalry and excludability create four possible types of goods, as shown in Table 1.1.

TABLE 1.1 Types of Goods

	Excludable	Non-Excludable
Rival	Private goods (food, clothing, housing)	Common goods (fish stocks, timber)
Non-rival	Club goods (social clubs, satellite television)	Public goods (air, lighthouses)

Much of human knowledge is in the public domain and can be considered a public good. This presents problems for free market economies, because if goods are to be freely available (non-excludable) and shared without competition (non-rival), it is hard to capture enough revenue to provide them. Fundamental research is therefore often supported by government funding. But knowledge does not always have to be provided as a public good. Two mechanisms exist to allow those who generate knowledge to acquire revenue from it: intellectual property rights (patents and copyright), and secrecy (trade secrets and confidentiality agreements). An example we will encounter in the following chapters is the credit risk score, which is knowledge about a customer sold as a club good, like satellite television.

By characterizing ideas and knowledge as non-rival, partially excludable goods, and describing them with endogenous variables in their economic models, Paul Romer[7] and Robert Lucas[8] have developed a New Growth Theory based on human capital rather than physical capital. In this theory growth is largely accounted for by two factors: (1) the general increase in the quantity of ideas, and (2) the extent of communication of those ideas, including the availability of knowledge to be bought and used by businesses in their operations. In other words, it is not labor or capital but rather the flourishing of human knowledge that is responsible for the growth of economies and the resulting improvements in human welfare.

The Knowledge Economy

The examples used by economists often characterize knowledge as *manufacturing technology*; they interpret the growth of knowledge as the ability to create new physical goods more efficiently. This is undeniably important, but an increasing proportion of businesses, for example the entire financial sector, do not process objects at all; they process only information. Such industries are built on *information technology*, which allows knowledge to be applied directly in making better decisions with the available information. No business sector is better placed to participate in global economic growth, provided businesses exploit the opportunities presented by the new knowledge-based decision-making technology. As Tom Debevoise has observed:

> Business Processes built entirely on the backs of obsolete models will not create future economic growth and profits. . . . More subtly, business process built without the benefit of knowledge-based decisions cannot keep their business profitable. Moreover, most processes are unstable and have been constructed with multiple outdated assumptions. This is little comfort for the many firms that seek to preserve the knowledge of the retiring baby boomer. "Knowledge" and the "creation of new knowledge" in all its domains and forms are the key critical success factors in all modern firms. Knowledge needs to be identified, defined, and incorporated into the decisions that create and maintain agile enterprise structures. In turn, these knowledge-driven business processes produce timely products, services, and profits.[9]

So we already have a functioning knowledge economy in which knowledge may be bought and sold, information technology enables knowledge-based decisions in knowledge-driven business processes, and global economic growth is ultimately fueled by the accumulation and distribution of knowledge. But in one respect, considered as a saleable product, most knowledge is still as primitive as a flint arrowhead: It has to be created using labor-intensive human processes. Universities and research centers are not factories of knowledge; they are workshops, and the rate of production of knowledge is limited by the productivity of the individual knowledge craftsmen.

But that is beginning to change, with the emergence of *machine learning*: a group of technologies including text mining, rule induction, and predictive analytics (to be discussed in Chapter 3). Machine learning is essentially a process for creating knowledge automatically from data. Until quite recently, this technology was highly specialized and used only by expert statisticians, but now it is available to the ordinary business user. Businesses now generate their own knowledge automatically and apply it in making automated business decisions. For example, a credit card company analyzes the behavior of its existing customers to produce predictive models that are then used in making automatic decisions on credit limits and interest rates for new applicants. Such models are a form of knowledge that is not "off the shelf," but specific to particular markets, products, and operating methods. The competitive advantage this brings to the company is protected by keeping the knowledge secret.

Turning back to Romer for a final word on the economics and a little star-gazing:

> Perhaps the most important ideas of all are meta-ideas. These are ideas about how to support the production and transmission of other ideas. The British invented patents and copyrights in the seventeenth century. North Americans invented the modern research university and the agricultural extension service in the nineteenth century, and peer-reviewed competitive grants for basic research in the twentieth century. . . . We do not know what the next major idea about how to support ideas will be. Nor do we know where it will emerge. There are, however, two safe predictions. First, the country that takes the lead in the twenty-first century will be the one that implements an innovation that more effectively supports the production of new ideas in the private sector. Second, new meta-ideas of this kind will be found.[10]

One exciting meta-idea of the twenty-first century will be machine learning: the automatic generation of knowledge from data. This will have huge ramifications in science and government as well as in business, where it will be used in automatic business decision-making. The effects this will have on the acceleration of growth are hard to predict, but they will be profound, especially as the quantity of available data explodes.

 ## THE KNOWLEDGEABLE BUSINESS

Now I want to focus in on the central subject of this book: decision management, which is an important aspect of the burgeoning knowledge economy. Decision management is the use of machine learning and automated decision-making to improve the profitability of business decisions. Knowledge does not just generate aggregate value at the macroeconomic level but specific value for an individual business, and it is possible to measure that value. Knowledge is used in making business decisions, and those decisions influence the profitability of the business.

Strategic versus Operational Decision-Making

James Taylor points out that not all decisions are of equal weight or value, and it is worthwhile to categorize them:[11]

■ High-value decisions can be characterized as *strategic*. Strategic decisions are made only by the board of directors or senior executives. They include, for example, mergers and acquisitions, investment and divestment, workforce resizing, and market positioning. The influence of such decisions on the company bottom line may be measured in millions or even billions of dollars.

■ Low-value decisions can be characterized as *operational*. Operational decisions are made by frontline staff in direct contact with customers. They include product selection; cross-, up-, and down-selling; and approval or rejection of applications. The influence of a single operational decision is probably measured in dollars, sometimes only cents.

Between these two extremes there is, of course, a spectrum of mid-value decisions, made by middle management and backroom teams such as analytics, research, and development. These mid-value decisions include product development, pricing, and marketing.

There is an interesting set of relationships between the value of a decision, the frequency with which it is made, and the amount of data and knowledge required to make the decision.

Strategic decisions are high-value and are made quite rarely. The board of directors may meet only once a month and may make decisions of significant value only a few times a year. But strategic decisions require enormous quantities of information. The background for a single acquisition decision will include stacks of company reports and accounts, product descriptions, market assessments, and biographies of the most important personnel. The executive team making the decision will be using complex financial and business models and applying many years of education and personal experience, along with detailed knowledge of the relevant corporate and accounting law.

In contrast, the frontline staff makes low-value operational decisions in the thousands or millions, every day. Each operational decision usually concerns a single case or event, often using information collected directly from the customer (for example, in an application form or claim form), so the quantity of data available for making the decision is limited. The knowledge brought to bear on the decision is limited, too; operational decisions tend to follow fairly strict company policies and guidelines, and the training required for frontline staff is typically on the order of months rather than years.

These relationships are summarized in Table 1.2.

There are two important observations to be made about these relationships. First, the value to the company of an individual decision reflects the

TABLE 1.2 Strategic and Operational Decisions

Level of Decision	Individual Value	Frequency	Data Required	Knowledge Required
Strategic	High	Low	High	High
Operational	Low	High	Low	Low

quantity of knowledge used to make it. Second—as first pointed out by Frank Rhode[12]—although the individual value of operational decisions may be small, their total value when combined may be comparable to that of strategic decisions. This means a company should pay as much attention to its operational decisions as it does to its strategic decisions.

As shown in later chapters, the investment required to automate any decision is determined almost entirely by the quantity of knowledge and data required to make that decision. So the implications for return on investment at the different levels of decision-making are clear. The cost of investment will be higher for strategic decisions, lower for operational decisions. But the return on automating operational decisions can be as high as that for strategic decisions. The return scales with the frequency of the decision, but the cost of investment does not, because the same business knowledge is applied to all cases.

Operational decisions, therefore, present the low-hanging fruit for decision management. Strategic decisions are instead supported by the field of business intelligence: a set of technologies for aggregating, analyzing, filtering, and presenting data to assist executives in their decision-making without actually making their decisions for them.

Strategic and Operational Decisions

Strategic decisions are infrequently made, high-value decisions, and are made by senior executives. They involve a large amount of data and a large amount of business knowledge and are, therefore, difficult and costly to automate.

Operational decisions are frequently made, low-value decisions, and are the responsibility of frontline staff. They involve a relatively small amount of data and a relatively small amount of business knowledge and are, therefore, relatively simple and inexpensive to automate. ■

Decision Yield

So far I have been using the term *value* in a very general way. How, specifically, does the encapsulation of business knowledge in an automated operational decision actually generate value for a company? To predict and measure return on investment (ROI) on decision management projects, Fair Isaac Corporation (FICO) has developed an approach called *decision yield*, which evaluates decision-making performance on five dimensions: precision, cost, speed, agility, and consistency:

> **Precision:** The effectiveness of the decisions you execute in your marketing and customer management systems, your call centers, and your branch offices. Measures include financial outcomes such as profit, customer lifetime value, revenue, losses, and cost relative to expected outcomes.
>
> **Cost:** The efficiency of your decision-making with regard to the expenses of executing decisions. Measures include activity-based costing, the cost of data elements needed to execute decisions (scores, credit bureau reports, motor vehicle reports, demographics), the cost of system resources, and other costs (for example, mail costs).
>
> **Speed:** How quickly you can execute decisions. Measures include indicators such as elapsed time between request and fulfillment, number of customers lost due to turnaround time, elapsed time for batch campaign runs.
>
> **Agility:** How quickly and easily you can change decision strategies within your systems and organizational infrastructure. Measures include how long it takes a business manager to change the rules or strategy from design through testing and implementation, how many resources need to be applied to change a decision strategy, and how quickly new information can be brought to bear on a decision strategy.
>
> **Consistency:** How well integrated and coordinated your decisions are across the enterprise. Measures include consistency over time, across channels, and within and across product lines.
>
> —Adapted from "How to Assess Your Decision Yield,"
> FICO Executive Brief 1961EX (2009)

The performance of a decision process across these five dimensions may be plotted graphically on a radar chart, before and after any investment in decision management, to give a holistic view of the benefits to the organization of the investment (see Figure 1.2). The differences between the "before" and "after" profiles give a qualitative measure of ROI.

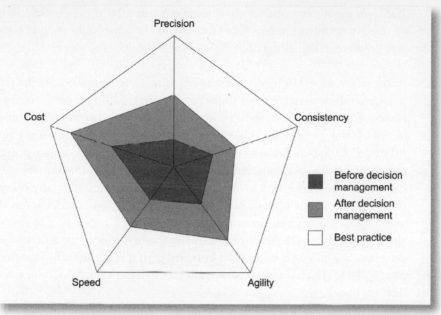

FIGURE 1.2   Decision Yield

This dimensions used in this figure neatly summarize the key benefits of decision management. All of these benefits arise from the ability to represent business knowledge in systems that automate business decision-making. That is such an important statement I'm going to say it again with more words, and in italics: *all of the benefits of decision management result from the ability to create explicit knowledge concerning business decision-making and to encapsulate that knowledge in systems that automate the decision-making.*

Decision Yield: The Benefits of Decision Management

Precision: Achieving accurate, reliable, and optimal decision-making on every case processed.

Cost: Reducing the operational costs of processing each case.

Speed: Reducing the time taken to process each case.

Agility: Allowing business strategy to be updated quickly and easily by business users.

Consistency: Ensuring a consistent set of business policies are applied across all channels, products, and cases. ■

The tools and techniques for creating and encapsulating knowledge will be described in detail in Chapter 3, but for now here's a brief indication of how they are involved in achieving each dimension of the decision yield:

- *Increased precision.* Decisions automated using decision management systems are more accurate than those made with traditional decision processes because they are based on knowledge in the form of rules or analytic models. If the systems are rule-based, they simulate the decision-making behavior of the best decision makers in your organization or guarantee that legislation is never unintentionally breached. If they are model-based, they make their decisions so as to optimize expected profit or any other measure important to your business. However implemented, they will apply the same optimal decision-making strategy consistently to every single case processed. And by monitoring the behavior of an automated decision, you can ensure that the knowledge in it is continually updated or adapted to the changing business climate so that performance does not degrade over time.

- *Decreased cost.* Using business knowledge to automate decision-making, rather than just administration, allows you to make profound changes in how you use your workforce. It may be possible to handle a large proportion of your cases entirely automatically, leaving human attention to be focused on difficult, risky, or possibly fraudulent cases. It also allows more flexibility in purchasing data; for example, deciding for each case whether bureau data are required and if so, which data would be useful and from which bureau they should be obtained.

- *Increased speed.* Even when using the best designed decision support system, a human decision maker will take seconds or minutes to make a basic accept/reject decision on a case, and possibly hours to make a complex decision like calculating the benefits due on a health insurance claim. When their business knowledge is captured and automated, the same decisions can be made in milliseconds. Online processing of applications for retail financial products such as credit cards is only possible because decision management enables a fully automated end-to-end originations process.

- *Increased agility.* When business knowledge resides in the heads of human decision makers, a change in company strategy requires, at the very least, circulation of new documentation and possibly retraining of staff, a process that can take days or weeks. When the decision is automated using a modern decision management tool, the business knowledge can be directly updated by managers without a conventional IT development and change management cycle. For example, a credit risk manager can change the criteria used to grade applicants by updating a table, test the new strategy against a simulated market, and deploy the new strategy to replace the current one, in a matter of minutes.

- *Increased consistency.* Once business knowledge has been captured and encapsulated in automated decisions, it can be reused across multiple products, lines of business, channels, and market sectors. This guarantees consistency of treatment of all your customers, as well as reducing implementation costs and simplifying maintenance. It also makes it easier to cross-sell between products or deal with product portfolios, rather than individual product-specific processes.

The decision yield diagram shown in Figure 1.2 provides a multidimensional and qualitative view of decision performance and the possibilities for improvement. To convert this to a single monetary value (for example, to provide hard ROI figures to support a business case), the business needs to agree on a method, based on corporate key performance indicators, to convert each qualitative dimension into dollars (or your preferred currency) so that the results can be summed.

This is not too hard for precision and cost, because they are already essentially financial measures. Speed and agility can be accounted partly as reduced lost opportunity costs (for example, for agility, if the typical benefit of updating your decision strategy is x per month in increased profit, and decision management allows you to reduce the time taken to implement the change from six months to one month, you will save $5x$ per strategy update). The consistency dimension can prove more problematic, because the returns are more abstract benefits such as customer experience and brand integrity. If these are to be included in the ROI figure the business needs to estimate what such benefits are actually worth in terms of (for example) customer loyalty and cross-sell opportunities.

My purpose here is not to provide a tutorial on the decision yield method; for a detailed description of this approach you should read Taylor[13] or Larry Rosenberger and John Nash.[14] Besides, other approaches to auditing the benefits of decision management projects could be equally valid. The point is to show that when business knowledge is embedded in automated decision-making systems, there is a range of specific benefits to the company that can be measured in dollars per year.

The value of those benefits is the value of the knowledge.

NOTES

1. R. M. Solow, "A Contribution to the Theory of Economic Growth," *Quarterly Journal of Economics* 70, no. 1 (1956): 65–94.
2. T. W. Swan, "Economic Growth and Capital Accumulation," *The Economic Record* 32 (November 1956): 334–361.
3. R. M. Solow, "Technical Change and the Aggregate Production Function," *Review of Economics and Statistics* 39 (1957): 312–320.
4. R. E. Lucas, Jr., "On the Mechanics of Economic Development," *Journal of Monetary Economics* 22 (January 1988): 3–42.
5. C. I. Jones and P. M. Romer, "The New Kaldor Facts: Ideas, Institutions, Population, and Human Capital," National Bureau of Economic Research Working Paper 15094 (2009).
6. P. M. Romer, Stanford University web page: www.stanford.edu/~promer/new_bio.html (May 2011).
7. P. M. Romer, "Increasing Returns and Long-Run Growth," *Journal of Political Economy* 94 (October 1986): 1002–1037; and P. M. Romer, "Endogenous Technological Change," *Journal of Political Economy* 98, no. 5 (October 1990): S71–S102.
8. Lucas, "On the Mechanics of Economic Development."
9. T. Debevoise, "Business Agility and a Meta-Knowledge Framework," blog posted November 7, 2010, www.tomdebevoise.com.
10. P. M. Romer, "Economic Growth," *The Concise Encyclopedia of Economics*, ed. David R. Henderson, (Liberty Fund, 2007).
11. J. Taylor, *Smart (Enough) Systems: How to Deliver Competitive Advantage by Automating Hidden Decisions* (Boston: Pearson Education Inc., 2007).
12. F. Rhode, "Little Decisions Add Up," *Harvard Business Review* (June 2005).
13. Taylor, *Smart (Enough) Systems*.
14. L. E. Rosenberger and J. Nash, *The Deciding Factor: The Power of Analytics to Make Every Decision a Winner* (San Francisco: Jossey-Bass, 2009).

2

Decisions in the Business Process

D ECISION MANAGEMENT REALIZES the value of business knowledge by using it to automate operational decisions. So, at first glance, you might think that a decision management project consists of three tasks: identify operational decisions in the business processes, codify the knowledge used to make them, and encapsulate the knowledge in automated decision-making systems. Unfortunately it is not quite as simple as that.

One reason is that the goal of decision management is to improve decision-making, not simply to automate the current process. Collecting existing business rules simply describes what is currently occurring in the business. This may be useful in the analysis of the efficiency of the current process or as a starting point for automation but will rarely be enough in itself.

A second, more subtle reason is that automation will inevitably change the business process around each decision being automated. To assess the costs and benefits of decision management we therefore need to look at the *whole process* before and after automation. This means that the disciplines of decision management and business process management are intimately related. Two common mistakes are (1) attempting to automate decision-making tasks without redesigning the surrounding business process, and (2) redesigning a business process without considering how the decision-making will be automated.

Decision management should always be considered both *during* process redesign and *as a form of* process redesign.

This chapter looks at how business processes may be modeled and redesigned using automated decision services to replace and restructure parts of the process workflow.

 ## BUSINESS PROCESS MODELING

Business process management (BPM) is the professional discipline concerned with designing and implementing business processes to maximize their value to the organization. A business process may be considered to be an interrelated set of activities performed by an organization to achieve its goals. Each of those activities can be carried out by people (such as employees) or technology (such as computer systems), or more commonly by some combination of the two.

Business process modeling specifies the constituent activities of a process and shows how these activities are related to one another. The specification of a process model is crucial to the acceptable performance of a process, in particular to the degree of repeatability that the process exhibits across time and participants. It is also important in determining how business processes generate value for the organization and how people or systems contribute to that value when they carry out activities in those business processes. Models are usually represented as diagrams in which sequences of activities are linked together to form process flows. There are a number of diagrammatic notations for modeling business processes; for the examples in this chapter I have used Business Process Modeling Notation (BPMN) 2.0, defined by the Object Management Group (OMG).[1]

Process modeling often involves decomposing business activities through several layers of detail. Activities in the top-level processes are typically very broad and may describe functions of whole departments or groups. Such high-level activities can be decomposed into *subprocesses* of smaller activities. These smaller activities can themselves be decomposed into subprocesses, and so on until atomic activities are reached: individual tasks that cannot be decomposed any further.

Once a process has been modeled in sufficient detail it is possible to enact it using a business process management system (BPMS): a computer system that controls the sequences of activities defined in the process model, automatically triggering those activities that are carried out by systems, and mediating those activities involving people (for instance, by providing user interface screens or sending items to people's work queues). An important feature of BPMN is that it is *executable*. It is possible to build a BPMS that uses the process models directly to manage processes, ensuring that the sequence of activities carried out for any particular case complies with the process specified in the model.

Note that BPMS is all about controlling sequences of activities; almost all the actual processing is carried out in services called from the process flow, not in the flow itself. This is why the role of the BPMS is sometimes referred to as "orchestration"; it is coordinating the services and ensuring that the right data are passed between them at the right times. This viewpoint is important in understanding how decision-making can be managed within business processes.

Business Process Modeling

A *business process model* specifies a business process as a sequence of *activities* that can be drawn in a *process flow diagram*.

BPMN (Business Process Modeling Notation) is one standard formalism for business process models as defined by the OMG.

A *BPMS* (business process management system) is a computer system that manages a business process by executing the sequence of activities defined in a business process model. ■

DECISION POINTS AND DECISION SERVICES

Decision management involves introducing automated decision-making into the process, so we need some way to represent this decision-making in the process model. BPMN 2.0 conveniently includes a special "business rule" task for this (see the *Decide eligibility* task in Figure 2.1). This task symbol represents a *decision point*: a point in the business process at which business knowledge is applied automatically to make a decision. The business rule task is atomic—it cannot be decomposed any further—and involves no user interaction. Note that although the business knowledge may be valid over a considerable period of time, any decision made using that knowledge is made at a single point in time using the case data available at that time.

The most common approach when automating operational decisions is to encapsulate the knowledge required for the decisions in decision services, which are called by the BPMS at the decision points in the process. A decision service takes a set of data describing a case and returns one or more decisions on the case by applying some business knowledge. These decision results can be used by the BPMS to route the case appropriately through the process flow and can be passed as data into other services.

Decision Points and Decision Services

A *decision point* is a point in the business process at which business knowledge is applied automatically to make a decision.

A *decision service* takes a set of data describing a case and makes one or more decisions on the case, by applying some encapsulated business knowledge.

Decision services are called by the BPMS at the decision points in the business process. Usually, one decision point is implemented using a single decision service, but a decision service may be called from multiple decision points. ■

So, for example, Figure 2.1 shows a simple process to handle an application for life insurance through a sales agent, who, for the purpose of this flow, is the user. The first activity is a user task to collect some data from the applicant. The next task is a decision point: *Decide eligibility*. To execute this task, the BPMS sends the application data to the *Decide eligibility* decision service, and receives back an eligibility decision (eligible or ineligible), and a set of reasons explaining the decision. The BPMS uses the result of the eligibility decision to determine the next activity. If the application is ineligible, the BPMS initiates a user task to inform the applicant that he or she has been declined using the reasons provided by the decision service to explain why. If the application is eligible, the BPMS invokes a subprocess to complete the sale.

A more typical process would have several decision points. Each decision point in the process flow calls only one decision service, but a decision service may be called from multiple decision points. That is, the same service may be reused to make decisions at several points in a business process or from multiple processes. This is not just a form of economy but a reliable way to enforce consistency of decision-making across different stages in the process, different product lines, different channels, and different functions in the business.

The decision services I will be considering in this book are *stateless*; that is, they have no memory. Goldfish-like, after the service returns the decision

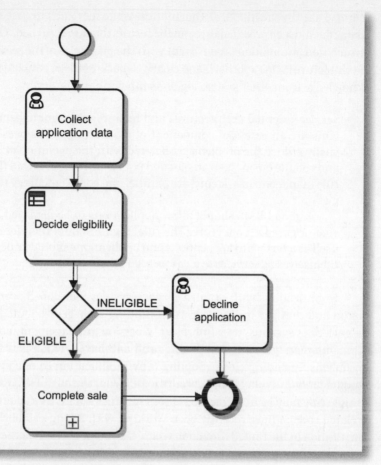

FIGURE 2.1 A Process with One Decision Point

results for a case, it forgets all about it. If it is called again with the same data it will make *exactly* the same decisions. The state of the case—its current position in the process flow, all the data collected so far, and all the decisions made—must either be maintained in the BPMS or "persisted" by using a service to write it away somewhere safe like a database. It is possible to create "stateful" decision services, but these present a number of challenges, technical and logical, and are not covered by the methodology proposed here.

The technologies used to create, deploy, and execute decision services will be covered in Chapter 3. But from the perspective of the BPMS, the technology used to implement any particular decision service is irrelevant. Like any other service used by the BPMS, all that matters is the service's *interface signature*: the data that must be provided to it and the results that are returned. This approach to decision automation is consistent with the principles of the service-oriented architecture (SOA) approach and clearly separates the organization's business knowledge from other system logic. As Ian Graham observes:

> Service-oriented architectures and business rules management systems are an essential component of modern agile businesses. They vastly reduce the problems associated with the evolution of complex and volatile business strategies and policies. SOA and BRMS [business rule management systems] are parallel and complementary technologies.
>
> A good BRMS should allow applications to be deployed in a service-oriented architecture. The rule engine should therefore present itself as a service to applications and applications should be deployable themselves as services (e.g., as web services).[2]

Organizations with extensive legacy systems developed over many years often find that key business decision-making logic is distributed throughout a variety of systems: user interfaces, workflow management, customer relationship management, accounting, and databases. This results in a host of problems, including close-coupling (any modification to one system entails modifications to others) and obscure logic (what the business considers to be a single rule may be implemented across several systems as a spaghetti of interrelated code). I have recently been working with a long-established financial institution in the United Kingdom, where the major obstacle to the introduction of decision management was that the existing legacy systems were so complex and intertwined, *nobody* knew exactly how they worked. The concept of the decision service provides a clean, manageable alternative.

 ## REDESIGNING PROCESS DECISIONS

When redesigning business processes to use decision services it is important to consider decision management as an integral part of the task of process modeling. Decision-making in the existing process is often distributed across people or time, and process redesign provides a unique opportunity to consolidate it. The goal of a good process design is to define a set of decision services that are efficient, independent, and reusable. Each of these characteristics has implications for how we should use decision services in our redesigned process.

Goals for Decision Service Design

1. Efficiency

   ■ Combine decision-making into a small number of services.

   ■ Present decision services only with the data they require.

   ■ Do not call decision services multiple times with the same data.

2. Independence

   ■ Divide decision-making naturally between decision services.

   ■ Minimize interaction between decision services.

3. Reusability

   ■ Generalize decision services for reuse across functions, channels, and products.

   ■ Reuse knowledge by encapsulating it in multiple decision services. ■

Efficiency: Much of the computational cost of calling a decision service is incurred in the interface—marshalling the input data, starting the service, and returning the results—rather than in actually making the decisions within the service. This means:

- Decision-making should be combined into a small number of services rather than split into many separate services.
- Decision services should be presented only with the data they require for the decisions they make.
- Decision services should not be called multiple times with the same case data.

Independence: A clean design is important both for the systems developers and for the business users who will have to express and maintain the knowledge encapsulated in the services. Business knowledge has a natural structure that should be reflected in the structure of the design. This means:

- Each decision service should carry out a natural component of decision-making, encapsulating a coherent body of business knowledge.
- Interaction between decision services should be minimized and limited to the use of previous results in making subsequent decisions.

Reusability: There are numerous benefits to the organization in achieving consistency of decision-making across functions, channels, and lines of business. The simplest means of achieving consistency is to share common decision services, but it is also possible to reuse decision components across services. This means:

■ Decision services should be generalized and reused rather than differentiated across functions, channels, and lines of business.
■ Where whole decision services cannot be reused, their behavior should be invented in such a way as to allow reuse of the knowledge encapsulated within them.

These goals should be in our minds as we embark on the task of automating the decisions in a business process. This task has three principal stages:

1. Build an abstract model of organizational decision-making.
2. Reallocate human roles around automated decision services.
3. Rationalize the decision points and the business process.

Modeling Human Decision-Making

We must not underestimate the complexity of human decision-making in any organization. Manually processing a single case will entail a spider's web of human interactions, possibly including case meetings, requests for advice, referrals to specialists, multiple levels of approval, oversight by managers, and many other exchanges of information. Somehow, out of this complex set of human activities and interactions emerges an agreed-upon set of decisions on the case. If we are to redesign such a complex decision-making process we first need to understand it.

Paul Konnersman has proposed an approach to analysis and modeling of human decision-making processes that can greatly simplify this apparently impossible task.[3] His Decision Process Specification method is based on the insight that since many decisions involve several people, the atomic activity to be modeled is the decision itself, not the work contribution of any particular person involved with it. In his approach, each decision is described as an activity involving one or more people in different roles. Konnersman uses five roles: every activity has a decision manager, but it may also have consultees, approvers, inspectors, and informees (see Table 2.1).

TABLE 2.1 Decision Roles in Decision Process Specification

Role	Responsible to	Responsible for
Decision manager: Manage the decision process, make the decision, and take responsibility for its implementation	The organization	Providing a timely, efficient, and effective decision-making and implementation process
	Consultees	Providing an opportunity to influence the decision before it is made
	Approvers	Submitting the decision for approval after it has been made but before any commitment is made to implementation
	Informees	Providing timely notification of the decision made after it has been made
Consultee: Provide either expertise required to make a good decision or the commitment of resources needed for its successful implementation (can influence but cannot veto)	The organization	Contributing expertise and resources that will improve the decision or its implementation
	Decision manager	Adhering to the decision process, providing decision manager with relevant expertise, taking responsibility for influencing the decision, and accepting the result when an opportunity to influence has been provided
Approver: Prevent organizationally intolerable outcomes that might result from a decision made without the benefit of expertise that is not otherwise available to the decision manager and assure that the decision has not been unduly influenced by the parochial interests of the decision manager to the detriment of the organization (can veto)	The organization	Assuring that the decision manager has not made a decision that favors parochial interests at the expense of the organization's welfare or that will expose the organization to unacceptable risk.
	Decision manager	Making the requirements for decision approval as clear and as specific as possible before the decision process begins, and providing timely notification of approval or disapproval with the reasons for any disapproval
Inspector: Ensure the decision result conforms to an established specification (can reject)	The organization	Assuring that the decision result conforms to all established specifications
	Decision manager	Assuring that the decision manager is aware of the result specifications before the decision is made and informing the decision manager of the inspection results (including the reasons for any failure to pass inspection) as soon as possible after the decision has been made
Informee: Implement the decision	The organization	Making all subsequent decisions and performing all subsequent tasks in a manner that is consistent with the decision made

Source: P. M. Konnersman, "Decision Process Specification: A Methodology for Modeling and Enacting Professional Work Processes." Working paper, 2006.

These roles interact with each other in ways that can be scripted. As a result, each decision has an internal process that depends on the set of roles potentially involved rather than the decision being made. Rather than modeling the particular variations of the decision process with the particular roles actually occurring, the abstract process with all possible participants in all roles is modeled once. Contributions to the decision by various people can then be represented simply as roles ("resources" in BPMN 2.0) rather than as multiple interacting activities. The simplification that this abstraction achieves can be seen even in the case of a decision involving only two roles: a decision manager and a single approver, as shown in Figure 2.2.

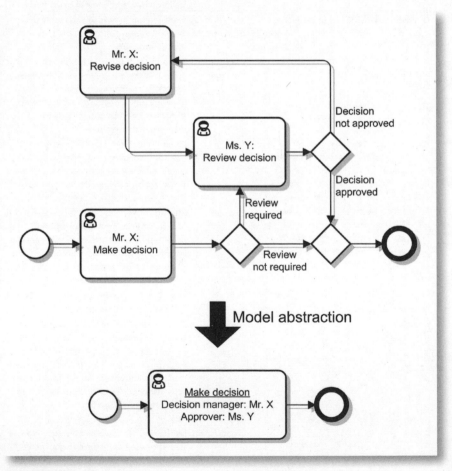

FIGURE 2.2 Model Abstraction Using Decision Roles

In this process, Mr. X makes a decision on the case. Depending on the properties of the case (for example, if its value is more than $10,000), this decision may have to be approved by Ms. Y. If Ms. Y does not approve of Mr. X's decision, he must revise it until she does. By modeling Mr. X as the decision manager and Ms. Y as the approver, this process can be abstracted to a single activity with two roles. The interaction between Mr. X and Ms. Y is treated as an internal process within the joint activity.

When more interacting roles are considered the internal processes can be much more complex and the simplification achieved through this abstraction even greater. As Konnersman points out:

> While the traditional approach works, it misses the opportunity to conceptually package the relationship between the decision maker and approver roles when they are associated with any decision. . . . The magnitude of the missed opportunity increases exponentially with the number of useful decision roles that can be identified.[4]

The result of this abstraction is a process model in which the network of human interactions comprising each decision—collaboration, approval, inspection, and so on—is represented as a single activity with multiple resources playing stereotypical roles. Konnersman's intent is to provide a way of modeling processes in which all activities are cast as decisions and to model decisions regardless of our ability to automate them. I am advocating his approach for a slightly different purpose. His analysis has value in process redesign in revealing the fundamental structure of the existing decision-making so that it can be accommodated within a new automated process that exploits knowledge-based decision services.

Automating Decision-Making

Chapter 1 introduced the concept of decision yield and described five dimensions of benefits that result from decision management. Precision, cost, speed, agility, and consistency can all be improved by replacing human decision-making with automated decision-making. One of the goals of process redesign should therefore be to use decision services wherever possible, using human tasks only to interact with the customer and to handle marginal and exceptional cases.

It is now widely accepted that this ideal of "straight-through processing" minimizes the time and effort needed to process a case (that is, it reduces cost and increases speed), but there is still a common misconception that this involves compromising the quality of decision-making, that there is some sort of trade-off between cost and quality. On the contrary: Automating decisions with decision management actually improves the precision and consistency of decision-making. It also improves agility, making it quicker and easier to modify the business policy enacted in the decisions.

However, moving decision services into the main process flow dramatically changes the roles that people perform in decision-making. Change management is often treated almost as an afterthought; the process is redesigned, then staff are retrained as necessary to deal with their roles, which have changed almost incidentally as a side effect of the redesign. But from the viewpoint of decision automation it can be seen that the change in their roles is central to the redesign; indeed it can be said to be part of the *purpose* of the redesign. The capabilities of the staff involved, the retraining required, and the continuing support to be provided for the new roles should all be considered in the early stages of the project as part of the redesign. Not only do they impose constraints on the solution, they are key to the success of the project.

Change management tends to focus on the *how* of change rather than the *what*. For example, John Kotter prescribes a program of eight steps:

1. Create a sense of urgency.
2. Develop a guiding coalition.
3. Develop a vision for change.
4. Communicate the vision.
5. Empower broad-based action.
6. Generate short-term wins.
7. Don't let up.
8. Make it stick in the organizational culture.[5]

It is possible that many transformation efforts fail because of lack of vision, but it is also possible that in many cases the devil is in the detail: The nature of the changes is misconceived. Viewing the transformation from the point of view of the people involved—thinking, as they will, about how their roles will change—is crucial when designing a coherent and effective set of changes.

In our simple example of a decision with approval (Figure 2.2), Mr. X was the decision manager and Ms. Y was the approver. When this decision is automated as part of a straight-through process, a decision service takes the place of the decision manager, and X and Y become reviewers who handle only the more difficult or exceptional cases. Part of the task of redesigning this process is to decide how the responsibilities for case review will be shared between X and Y. One option would be to have X and Y provide two levels of review with different levels of authority. A table like Table 2.2 may be used to remap their roles.

TABLE 2.2 Remapping Roles in Decision with Approval

Participant	Role before Automation	Authority	Role after Automation	Authority
Ms. Y	Approver	Over $10K	Level 2 reviewer	Over $20K
Mr. X	Decision manager	Up to $10K	Level 1 reviewer	$10K–$20K
Decision service	None	None	Decision manager	Up to $10K

Both roles have changed in the straight-through process: Mr. X is now reviewing cases rather than carrying out the initial decision-making, and Ms. Y's level of authority is higher than before since Mr. X has taken responsibility for some of her reviews. Ideally, we should adopt a systematic remapping of roles across the organization, so that wherever we automate a decision of a certain type we use the same replacement roles, with a consistent approach to increasing the responsibilities of the people involved. Note that the decision service is included alongside our human staff as one of the participants in this remapping exercise and considered to have a level of authority. The role remapping step is shown in Figure 2.3.

Having used abstraction to produce a simplified model of the decision-making process, and remapped the roles of the participants in the decisions,

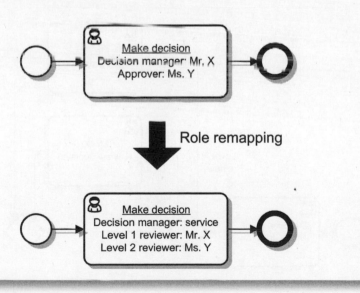

FIGURE 2.3 Role Remapping

we can now expand those decisions to reveal a full model of the automated process flow. Figure 2.4 shows the expanded model for our simple example: a human decision with approval has been replaced by an automatic decision with human review.

In this subprocess a decision service (modeled as a business rule task in BPMN 2.0) is making an automated decision on the case, as well as deciding on the level of review required by assessing the value of the case and referring to the authority levels in Table 2.2. Based on these decisions returned by the service, the BPMS either passes the case straight through without any human involvement or refers it for review. This simple pattern is very powerful, and

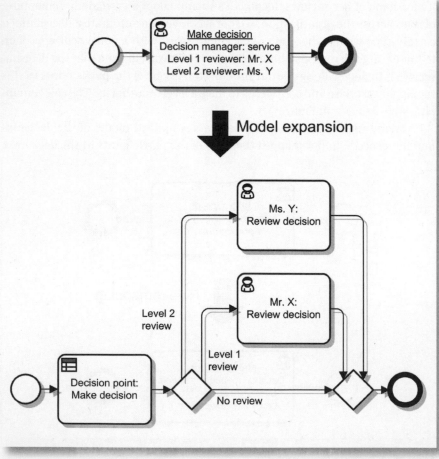

FIGURE 2.4 Model Expansion

is commonly used in straight-through processing with automated decision-making.

Rationalizing the Decision Points

The previous example focused on the abstraction, remapping, and expansion of a single decision. But the result of our analysis of the organizational decision-making will be a network of many decisions. When these are all abstracted, remapped, and expanded, the result will be a process flow including chains of many decision-making patterns such as the one seen in Figure 2.4. We should not stop here. Business process modeling is an opportunity for rationalization and simplification, aimed at achieving the goals previously discussed: efficiency, independence, and reusability of decision points.

Such rationalization requires some flexibility in the process. This flexibility is mostly provided by one simple principle: a decision can be taken at any point in the process between (a) the point at which all the data required by the decision are available from the process, and (b) the point at which the results provided by the decision are required by the process. It is therefore often possible to group decisions together into a smaller number of decision points.

As a simple example, Figure 2.5 shows a process containing two consecutive "decision with review" patterns: the first to check and review credit policy, the second to check and review fraud indicators. Each of these uses a decision point returning an accept/refer/decline decision that is used to route the case through the process. Both of these decisions are based on previously collected data; no new data are collected between the credit and fraud decisions. This means that the two decisions may be taken at a single decision point—*Check credit and fraud*—as shown in Figure 2.6.

After rationalizing the decision points, it is often the case that the remaining business process may be restructured and simplified, but our flexibility here is mainly constrained by organizational issues. For example, in Figure 2.6 there are two independent review tasks for credit and fraud, and these are executed in series in the process flow. This wastes process time; the credit and fraud teams are independent and could be working on the case in parallel as shown in Figure 2.7. However, this will sometimes result in the fraud team reviewing cases that would have been declined by the credit team, so we are trading process duration for process costs. The optimal design will depend on the referral rates and review costs, which differ markedly between business sectors and will be constrained by the resources available in the review teams.

Note that the decision point in Figure 2.6 returned two separate routing decisions for credit and fraud, but in Figure 2.7 these have been combined into

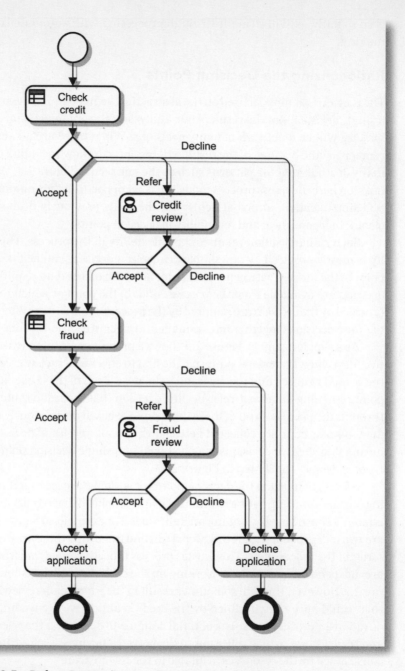

FIGURE 2.5 Before Rationalization: Two Decision Points

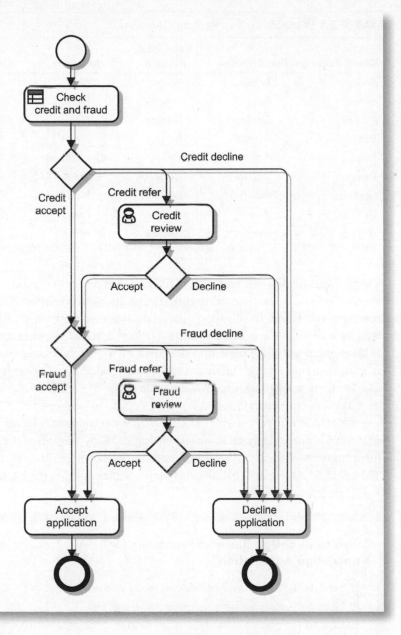

FIGURE 2.6 After Rationalization: A Single Decision Point

TABLE 2.3   Combining Two Routing Decisions

Credit Routing	Fraud Routing	Combined Routing	Referrals	Declines
Accept	Accept	Accept	None	None
Accept	Refer	Refer	Fraud	None
Accept	Decline	Decline	None	Fraud
Refer	Accept	Refer	Credit	None
Refer	Refer	Refer	Credit, fraud	None
Refer	Decline	Decline	Credit	Fraud
Decline	Accept	Decline	None	Credit
Decline	Refer	Decline	Fraud	Credit
Decline	Decline	Decline	None	Credit, fraud

a single routing decision and a list of referrals (credit and/or fraud). Table 2.3 shows the logic for restructuring these decisions, which relies on the natural precedence between the decision values: decline outweighs refer, which outweighs accept. The combined routing decision determines whether the case is accepted, referred for review, or declined; the referrals decision determines whether the case is reviewed by the credit team, fraud team, or both. Combining decisions in this way also provides a list of declines, but these are not used in the process shown in Figure 2.7.

This is just one very simple example of how decisions may be restructured without fundamentally changing their logic. Many scenarios are possible, including more complex cases using combinations of more than two decisions. The example is intended to illustrate two principles: (1) that the business logic

---

Steps to Redesign Business Processes for Knowledge Automation

1. Model the human decision-making using decision roles.
2. Remap the roles for automated decision-making.
3. Expand the decisions to reveal a full model of the automated process.
4. Rationalize the decision points.
5. Optimize the remaining business process.

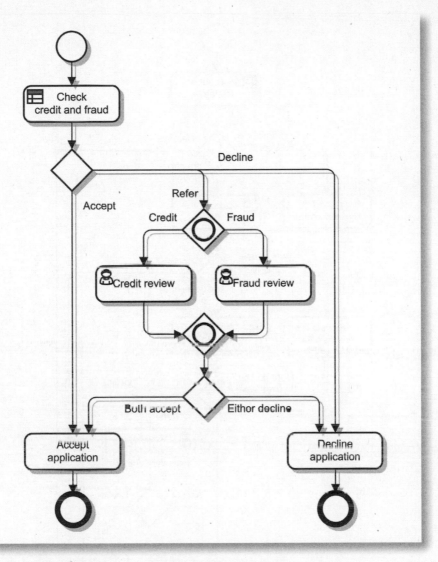

FIGURE 2.7 Optimizing the Remaining Business Process

for routing cases through the business process should be held in the decision service wherever possible rather than in the BPMS, and (2) that the vocabulary used in the definition of the logic should naturally reflect the structure of the process flow. To show these principles at work, I now describe a common process flow with its decision points and routing logic.

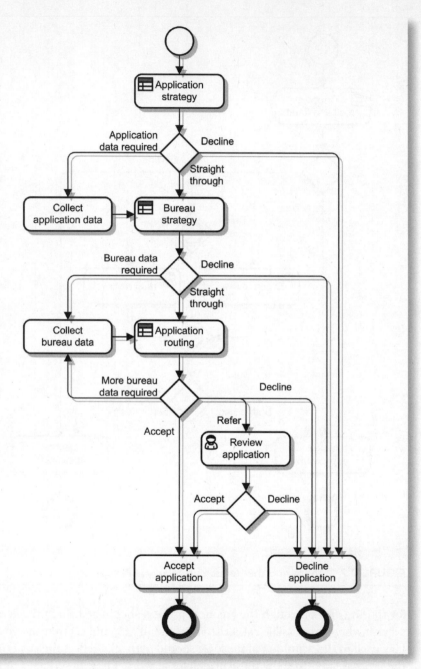

FIGURE 2.8 Typical Decision Points for Originations

ORIGINATIONS PROCESS TEMPLATE

The process shown in Figure 2.8 is a simplified template for an automated originations process for selling retail financial products such as credit cards and personal loans online. It has a straight-through processing flow for rapid closure on low-risk, high-value customers, side loops for data capture and human review, and multiple decline paths so that applications may be removed from the process as soon as they can be identified as undesirable. For clarity, activities such as data collection and review have been depicted as single tasks, although they will usually be more complex (as discussed earlier). I will return to this example process in later chapters when we look at the methodology for analyzing, specifying, and implementing decision services.

This type of process is typically automated with three principal decision services, which in this template I have named *Application strategy*, *Bureau strategy*, and *Application routing*.

The *Application strategy* decision service determines what type of application this is and, hence, what application data will be required. For example:

- If the applicant has received a preapproved offer through direct marketing, the case can be passed straight through without collecting any further application data.
- If the applicant is an existing customer who is currently in default, he or she can be immediately declined.
- If the applicant is an existing customer applying for an additional product, we need to know what product he or she is applying for but do not need to collect personal details.
- If the applicant is unknown to us we need to collect a full set of application data including personal details as well as the requested product.

The *Collect application data* task may then be used to collect the data specified by the *Application strategy* decision service through the appropriate channel (for example, by calling a sequence of selected user interface screens).

The *Bureau strategy* decision service uses the application data to decide which credit reference agencies should be used and what bureau data need to be purchased from them. The principal purpose of this decision point is to allow all the bureau data required for decision-making to be acquired at minimal cost. For example:

- If we already hold a full set of up-to-date bureau information on the applicant (this probably applies to all preapproved applications), the case can be passed straight through without collecting any further bureau data.
- If the application data are sufficient to show that the case is outside our lending policy for the requested product, the application can be declined.
- In other cases the service specifies which bureau data are required (for example, credit records, behavior scores, fraud indicators) and the preferred order for using the credit reference agencies.

The *Collect bureau data* task may then be used to collect the bureau data specified by the *Bureau strategy* decision service, calling the credit reference agencies in the order specified until all the required data have been acquired.

The *Application routing* decision service now has all the data it needs to decide how we should route this case and what offers, if any, should be made. This service encapsulates our corporate credit policy, typically covering product eligibility, credit risk, and affordability. For example:

- If the collected data do not allow a clear decision to be made, and the credit reference agencies listed by the *Bureau strategy* service have not all been used, more bureau data may be collected, and the *Application routing* service may be called again.
- If the application is clearly outside our lending criteria for the requested product and no down-sell is possible, the application can be declined.
- If either the requested product or a down-sell can be offered, the application can be accepted.
- If there are aspects of the case that require human inspection or judgment, the case can be referred for review.

The *Review application* task is a user task that allows an expert (for example, someone on the credit or fraud review team) to assess the case and decide on the outcome.

Either the *Accept application* task or the *Decline application* task completes the process, as determined by the *Application routing* decision service or the review team.

APPROACHES TO PROCESS DESIGN

In the design of any automated customer-facing process, such as the originations template in Figure 2.8, there is an interplay between three levels:

1. The customer journey, including the application process, feedback on progress, presentation of offers, and notification of the final decision.
2. The underlying business process with its activities of data collection, case review, and case closure.
3. The decision services, directing the progress of the case and allowing automation of decision-making.

The "outside-in" approach championed by Steve Towers stresses the importance of the customer journey, while traditional BPM focuses more on the underlying business process.[6] But when automating processes using decision management, these two goals—a clear structure for the customer's interaction and an efficient set of business processes—both depend on a clean design for the decision services. (As outlined earlier, this is one that achieves efficiency, independence, and reusability.)

In the following chapters, I describe three further levels of design below the decision services:

4. The structure of the decision-making within each decision point.
5. The specific knowledge (such as business rules) supporting each decision.
6. The implementation of the knowledge as executable software.

Levels of Design in Knowledge Automation

1. The customer journey
2. The business process
3. The decision services
4. The structure of decision-making
5. The encapsulated business knowledge
6. Executable software

The field contains similar differences in viewpoint on the merits of top-down and bottom-up approaches across these levels. The Decision Management approach as described by James Taylor and Neil Raden proposes an essentially top-down approach, starting with the definition of the business decisions to be made before identifying the business knowledge that enables them.[7] The Business Rules approach espoused by Ronald Ross and the Business Rules Group views the business rules as primary, representing generic constraints on how business may be conducted, and views the decision services as opportunities to enforce the rules.[8]

However, there is a lot of common ground, and these different viewpoints are largely a matter of emphasis rather than a substantial disagreement. So Ross, when comparing the dueling manifestos of these two camps, is conciliatory:

> The thinking in Enterprise Decision Management is that you shouldn't say "rule" when you mean "decision." In other words, it's some decision that rules can be used to make that provides the actual value-add for the business—not the rules per se. To say this differently, rules are simply the means to some important business end, some operational decision(s) to be made. So the EDM message is that you shouldn't talk to business executives about the means (rules) when it's the ends (decisions) that really matter. It's simply the wrong artifact.
>
> It's an excellent point. It's not rules per se that makes [sic] a company act smarter; it's enabling better decisions that makes the company act smarter. Rules and rule management are simply a means to that end. I'm very comfortable with that view and I think the message is a good one.[9]

The approach I take in this book is not radical; I suspect it is one with which most practitioners in the field would agree. When automating business processes, the approach should be broadly top-down, but the activities at each level must be guided and constrained by looking ahead to the needs and possibilities of the next level.

In the top three levels, a pure inside-out approach is not feasible; it is not possible to design a set of decision services in isolation, without first considering the user journey and business processes they are intended to serve. But a pure outside-in approach is not feasible either. When designing the user journey and business processes, it is vital to bear in mind that they will have to be implemented using a rational and efficient set of decision services. Realizing the benefits of decision management, therefore, depends on recognizing that *all three levels* are important and need to be considered together in the process design.

Similarly, as we move on to the next three levels I will propose a top-down process of analyzing the structure of decision-making at each decision point, discovering the knowledge required for each decision and then implementing it as software. But decision analysis and knowledge discovery must be guided and constrained; they must bear in mind the techniques that are available for the implementation of the knowledge if that implementation is to be efficient and maintainable. The approach we actually need is "top-down with look-ahead."

So, before addressing the core subject of this book—a methodology for decision analysis and knowledge discovery—I will describe the principal technologies for the encapsulation of business knowledge in decision services.

 NOTES

1. Object Management Group, *Business Process Model and Notation (BPMN) Version 2.0.* www.omg.org/spec/BPMN/2.0 (2011).
2. I. Graham, *Business Rules Management and Service Oriented Architecture: A Pattern Language* (Chichester, UK: John Wiley & Sons, 2006).
3. P. M. Konnersman, "Decision Process Specification: A Process for Defining Professional and Managerial Work Processes." *Portland International Conference on Management of Engineering and Technology,* July 27–31, 1997, Portland, Oregon.
4. P. M. Konnersman, *Decision Process Specification: A Methodology for Modeling and Enacting Professional Work Processes* (working paper, 2006).
5. J. P. Kotter, *Leading Change* (Boston: Harvard Business School Press, 1996).
6. S. Towers, *Outside-In: The Secret of the 21st Century Leading Companies* (BP Group Publishing, 2010).
7. J. Taylor, *Smart (Enough) Systems: How to Deliver Competitive Advantage by Automating Hidden Decisions* (Boston: Pearson Education Inc., 2007).
8. Ronald G. Ross, *Principles of Business Rule Approach* (Boston: Addison-Wesley, 2003).
9. Ronald G. Ross, "A Case of Dueling Manifestos? Business Rules and Enterprise Decision Management," *Business Rules Journal* 8, no. 8 (August 2007). www.BRCommunity.com/a2007/b357.html.

CHAPTER THREE

Encapsulating Knowledge in Decision Services

T HE DEFINING CHARACTERISTIC of the human species is language: the ability to communicate information between individuals using symbols agreed upon as part of a culture. Once our brains had evolved to be capable of symbolic gesture and speech, they were also capable of transmitting and preserving human knowledge in other symbolic forms. Human culture expanded to include saga and song, written language, pictures, maps, and diagrams. Culturally preserved knowledge had evolutionary value because it allowed one individual's successful behavior to be adopted by other individuals without those individuals ever meeting.

Even when the rewards are not survival or reproduction, knowledge continues to have practical or economic value because it enables people to *do* things. Using a map, I can find my way to places I have never visited before, which have been visited by the cartographers. Until very recently all such recorded knowledge was strictly a means of communication between two people: One person had to formulate the knowledge and another had to interpret it. Recently, however, new ways to represent knowledge have been invented that can dispense with one or both of these human agents:

- Some forms of knowledge do not need to be interpreted by a human being but can be executed directly by a machine. Using its machine-executable knowledge of the road network, your GPS navigation system can automatically find the best route to your destination and guide you along the journey.
- Some forms of knowledge can be generated by a machine. Much of the knowledge used by your GPS navigation system is compiled and updated semiautomatically from a variety of sources.

Automating decisions in business processes involves identifying or generating the business knowledge required to make those decisions and codifying it in a machine-executable form. The knowledge can then be automated by encapsulating it in services that execute the decisions.

This chapter briefly describes three technologies that are the forms of executable knowledge most commonly used to build decision services for business process automation: business rules, algorithms, and predictive analytic models. Business rules and algorithms are forms of knowledge that are machine executable but formulated by a human expert. Predictive analytics goes further: it allows machine-executable knowledge to be generated by a machine from historical data.

The type of software tool typically used to create, deploy, and execute decision services is often called a business rules management system (BRMS) or a business rule engine (BRE). Both terms are slightly misleading, because (as we will see) business rules are usually only part of the solution and sometimes quite a minor part. There is an old term that has passed out of fashion but that was much more accurate: knowledge-based system (KBS). This would cover any system that can model business knowledge and deploy it in a decision service. But it is more important to use terms that are currently used and understood by the industry, so I will use BRMS when talking about the systems that create and manage business knowledge and BRE when talking about the components or features of a BRMS that actually execute the knowledge.

Tools for Decision Services

A BRMS (business rules management system) is a software tool used to model business knowledge and deploy it as a decision service.

A BRE (business rules engine) is the component of a BRMS that actually executes the business knowledge in a decision service.

BRMS and BRE are capable of modeling and executing various forms of business knowledge: not just business rules but also algorithms and predictive analytic models. ■

BUSINESS RULES

A business rule is a logical statement that allows a conclusion to be drawn from a set of conditions. Rules are conventionally expressed in the form "IF <conditions> THEN <conclusion>." Below are some examples, all real business rules drawn from projects I have worked on in a variety of fields.

Many business rules for process automation are used to determine routing decisions such as those in the originations template in Chapter 2, for example:

- IF the client dispute indicator in the applicant's bureau report is "Y" THEN the application routing is "decline."
- IF the applicant is under debt counseling and the purpose of loan is consolidation THEN the application routing is "refer" and the referral type is "credit."
- IF the member's policy was cancelled prior to the date of the treatment or prior to the date of the admission to the hospital THEN the claim routing is "reject."
- IF the charge is for medical attendance and the doctor has not submitted Part 2 of a claim form indicating medical attendance in the treatment details section THEN the claim routing is "pend."

But rules can also be used for many other types of decision. Here is a potpourri:

- IF the date of the property valuation is more than 100 days before the date of application THEN the property valuation is unacceptable.
- IF the unsecured amount is less than the maximum unsecured amount and the loan-to-value ratio is less than the maximum loan-to-value ratio THEN the mortgage is secured.
- IF the application type is "scored" and the requested products include personal loan or credit card and the requested products do not include current account THEN cross-sell a current account.
- IF the credit card type is "platinum" and the credit limit is less than 2000 THEN down-sell to "classic" type.
- IF the applicant is an existing customer and the most recent bureau response is still valid and the most recent bureau score is not between 595 and 629 THEN the required bureau service level is "mini."

- IF the applicant is a new customer and the applicant employment status is contract worker or self-employed and the risk grade is less than 3 THEN the minimum deposit is 15 percent.
- IF the claim type is maternity and the condition code is 660 or 670 THEN the onset date is the date of admission minus 52 weeks.
- IF the procedure is MRI scan and the hospital is not listed as an approved MRI center in the Directory of Hospitals THEN the procedure is ineligible.

As these examples show, rules are discrete and independent statements that each express a single atom of executable business knowledge. By independent, I mean that the meaning of a rule is entirely contained within itself and does not depend on its relation with other rules. This is not true for "IF . . . THEN . . ." statements in a conventional programming language, because they are executed in sequence and removing or changing one statement may affect the behavior of all the subsequent statements. Business rules may be defined in such a way that their order (within a rule set) is irrelevant. This makes the task of expressing, implementing, and maintaining business knowledge much simpler, allowing it to be carried out by business domain experts and business analysts rather than IT development staff.

Only a brief introduction can be provided here. Useful texts on business rules include *Principles of the Business Rule Approach* by Ronald Ross,[1] *Business Rules Applied* by Barbara von Halle,[2] and *Business Rules Management and Service Oriented Architecture* by Ian Graham.[3]

Object Models

An important feature of business rules is that they are written using terms from a structured vocabulary known as an object model, fact model, or domain ontology. *Object model* is a very appropriate term, because it provides a model of the things to be referred to in the rules, a model that is crafted specifically for the domain of the knowledge. So for a set of business rules to adjudicate medical health insurance claims, the model would contain objects such as Claim, Procedure, Patient, Hospital, and Doctor.

A lot of logic concerning the natural relationships between these objects is held in the ontology rather than in the rules, for example, the fact that a Claim relates to one Patient undergoing a number of Procedures in a Hospital. The items of data referred to in the conditions and conclusions of rules are never simply variables but are always properties of objects, for example, the age of the Patient, or the date of the Procedure. This simplifies the rules and makes it possible to express them in something resembling natural language, making them comprehensible to business domain experts.

Object models support *inheritance*: the idea that one object can be a type or subclass of another object. For example, a Consultant might be defined as a type of Doctor. The Consultant object then inherits all the properties of the Doctor object, and may have further properties of its own. This would mean that Consultants can be described using all the terms that apply to Doctors (for example, specialty) but may also be described using terms that only apply to Consultants (for example, hospital affiliation and department).

The objects in an object model are more accurately described as *classes*, that is, they represent a set of items of a particular type. Classes support *instantiation*: any real example of an object is an *instance* of the class. Instances also inherit all the properties of their parent object. So my cat Mimi is an instance of the object Cat, which is a subclass of the object Animal, and so on.

Inference Strategies

Systems capable of executing such knowledge are called business rule engines. Each business rule permits the BRE to make a single logical inference: it can infer that the conclusions of the rule are true when the rule's conditions are satisfied. Some of these conditions may be evaluated directly using the values of input data, but others may depend on the conclusions of other rules. This means that rules form a logical network that may contain chains of several or many rules. Two principal types of inference are possible over such a network: forward chaining and backward chaining. Both of these strategies are supported to some extent in most commercially available BREs:

- In *forward chaining*, the BRE evaluates rules against an initial set of known facts, until it finds one whose conditions are satisfied. That rule is then said to "fire," which means that its conclusion is added to the set of known facts. The BRE continues to evaluate rules, adding the conclusions of any that fire, until no further inferences can be made. This strategy is also called "data directed," because reasoning starts from the initial data and proceeds through chains of inferences to the final conclusions. Forward chaining is the best approach when a fixed set of initial data is provided, and all the possible inferences from it are required. It is very common in the domains discussed in this book.

■ In *backward chaining*, the BRE sets out to establish the truth of a proposition. It does this by finding a rule that has that proposition as its conclusion and evaluating that rule to see whether its conditions are satisfied. If those conditions refer to the conclusions of other rules, those rules must be evaluated in turn, until the whole chain of reasoning is established. This strategy is also called "goal directed," because reasoning starts from the desired goal and proceeds through chains of inferences toward the supporting data. Backward chaining is more appropriate when data have to be obtained on demand (e.g., by asking questions of a user or querying an external database), and only certain conclusions are of interest. It is commonly used for diagnosis, where each hypothetical diagnosis is investigated and ruled out before considering the next.

These basic strategies are somewhat naïve, though, and would be very inefficient when applied to a knowledge base containing thousands of rules. Most BREs use highly sophisticated algorithms to optimize the speed of inference over large rule sets. The most important of these is Rete, which was developed by Charles Forgy.[4] Most BREs now support Rete or its later versions Rete II and Rete III. Essentially, Rete precompiles the rules into a network, expressing all their interdependencies, and uses that network to schedule rules optimally for evaluation. The network adjusts itself after every rule firing so that the rules scheduled for evaluation are only those that might fire, given what is currently known.

Rule Sets and Metaphors

Another means of achieving efficiency is to divide the rules into sets (the smaller the better), and only evaluate one set at a time. The logic for determining which rule set should be applied at any time may be defined by a higher-order set of rules or using a procedural flow diagram. There can then be a strong relationship between the rule sets and the decisions taken by the decision service: For example, each rule set takes one decision and contains only rules that contribute to that decision. This has benefits beyond efficiency. First, it allows reuse of knowledge at the rule set or decision level, rather than just the whole decision service. Second, it makes rule definition and maintenance simpler for the business domain experts. I address how to relate rule sets to decisions in the Chapters 4 and 6.

Once rules are organized into rule sets, they may be represented in other forms, or metaphors, for the convenience of business users. These include decision trees and decision tables.

Business Rules

A *business rule* is an atom of business knowledge, expressed in the form IF <conditions> THEN <conclusion>.

The conditions and conclusions of business rules refer to the properties of *objects* in an *object model*.

In *forward chaining*, the BRE evaluates rules whose conditions use the currently available data and adds their conclusions to the list of available data.

In *backward chaining*, the BRE evaluates rules whose conclusions are required and adds any unknown data in their conditions to the list of required conclusions.

Rules are organized into *rule sets*. All the rules in a rule set are involved in making the same decision.

Rule sets can be represented using *metaphors* such as decision tables and decision trees. ■

Decision Tables

If all the rules in a rule set have (a) conditions based on a small common set of input variables and (b) conclusions that determine the same output variables, they can conveniently be represented as a table. A decision table has a column for each property used in the conditions and a column for each property set in the conclusions. Each row in the table represents a business rule. When a rule does not use one or more of the condition properties, those cells are left empty or marked "not applicable."

The table format is easily understood by business users, and makes it easy to check that all scenarios have been covered. Behind the scenes, however, the BRE evaluates the table as a rule set and each row as a business rule. An example of a decision table is shown in Table 3.1. In this table, two conditions—mortgage product and contingency reserve percentage—are used to decide on two conclusions—credit quality and maximum loan-to-value (LTV).

Decision Trees

When the rules in a rule set share many of their conditions and determine the value of a single property, they can sometimes be conveniently represented as a tree. A decision tree classifies a case by a series of checks; each node in the tree tests a single property, and the branches out of it cover all the possible values

TABLE 3.1 A Decision Table

Conditions		Conclusions	
Mortgage Product	Contingency Reserve	Credit Quality	Maximum LTV
Y	> 30%	A	95%
Y	>20%, <=30%	B	75%
Y	>10%, <=20%	C	60%
Y	<= 10%	Decline	0%
N	> 25%	A	80%
N	<= 25%	Decline	0%

for that property. The terminal nodes (or "leaves" of the tree) are the possible classifications. The mapping to the underlying rules is less obvious than with the decision table: Each possible path through the tree is equivalent to a single rule, and each node along the path is one of the rule's conditions.

Decision trees are another format that is natural to business users, especially for logic that categorizes or segments a case. A simple decision tree is shown in Figure 3.1 (most trees would have more branches than this). This tree decides on the price band to be applied. It is equivalent to a rule set of 10 rules: one for each leaf node. One of these rules is:

- IF application type is new and segment is up-market and application score <= 745 THEN price band = C.

The path embodying this rule is marked with a heavy line.

Note that different tests, and different numbers of tests, are applied for different cases: new customers have their price band set according to segment and application score, existing customers have theirs set only by behavior score, and instant customers have theirs set by strategy code and behavior score. The tree is therefore said to be asymmetrical.

This property of symmetry in the rules determines whether a table or a tree is the most appropriate metaphor. Highly symmetrical rules (that is, rules that have a constant number of conditions based on the same shared variables) are naturally expressed as a table; highly asymmetrical rules cannot be expressed as a table without a lot of cells being marked as "not applicable," so should be expressed as a tree.

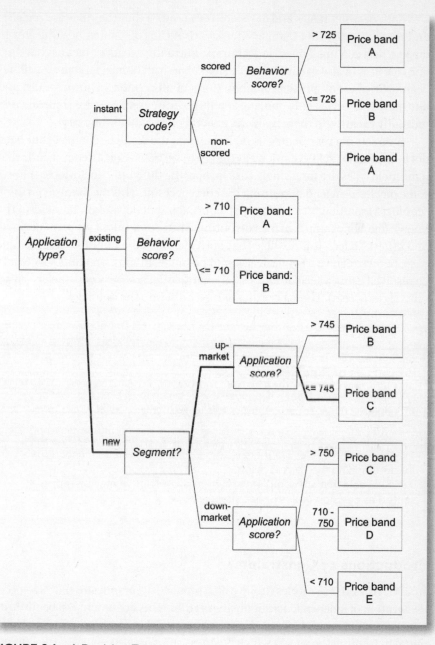

FIGURE 3.1 A Decision Tree

Both decision tables and decision trees require that the rules are *complete* and *mutually exclusive*. Complete means that the rules must be sufficient to make a decision in all possible scenarios; mutually exclusive means that only one rule fires in any particular scenario. Tables are complete if some result has been defined for all possible combinations of all possible column values and mutually exclusive if only one row applies to any case. Trees are complete and mutually exclusive if there is always exactly one result for any case.

Rule sets not represented as tables or trees must still be complete but need not be mutually exclusive so long as they are *consistent*. Consistency means that if multiple rules fire for a single case, proposing different conclusions, there is some mechanism for determining the correct result. This mechanism is called "conflict resolution." The particular approach will depend on domain of the knowledge. For example, in a set of routing rules, some might propose "decline" and others "refer." It is possible that both types of rule might fire for a single case, but we require a single decision to be made. In most domains this would be resolved using a set of priorities (for example decline outweighs refer, which outweighs accept). These priorities can be built into the ontology.

Properties of Rule Sets

A rule set is *complete* if it can make a decision in all possible scenarios. Rules in a rule set are *mutually exclusive* if only one rule fires under any scenario.

A rule set is *consistent* if either (a) the rules are mutually exclusive, or (b) when multiple rules fire there is some *conflict resolution* mechanism for determining the correct result.

Rule sets that are complete and mutually exclusive may be represented as decision tables or decision trees. ■

Productions or Constraints?

In 2002, the Business Rules Group (BRG) published a manifesto[5] that is a sort of declaration of independence for business rules. This document is a beautifully concise statement of the principles of business rules and has been very influential in framing the way in which business rules are perceived and discussed. I recommend it as a starting point if you are new to the concepts of business rules.

Although I agree wholeheartedly with most of the manifesto, there are two articles that I need to address, because they seem at first sight to be at odds with the approach I am taking in this book:

4.5. A rule is distinct from any enforcement defined for it. A rule and its enforcement are separate concerns.

4.6. Rules should be defined independently of responsibility for the who, where, when, or how of their enforcement.

The four example routing rules presented at the beginning of this Business Rules section are not in accordance with these two articles, because they combine business policies with the "how of their enforcement." BRG insists that business rules should be pure declarative constraints, with a separate "enforcement regime stating what the consequences would be if the rule were broken."[6] Let's look at the implications of this idea using our first example routing rule:

- IF the bureau client dispute indicator is "Y" THEN the application routing is "decline."

A rule expressed in this way is called a *production rule*, because when it is evaluated it produces a new item of data (in this case, a proposed value for the application routing). To recast this rule as a constraint, it could be stated as:

- At the date of application an applicant MUST NOT have a bureau report with client dispute indicator = "Y."

There would then have to be a separate enforcement rule stating that if this constraint is violated at the time of application, the applicant should be declined.

In my experience the need to consider abstract statements of business constraints arises very rarely. For most practical purposes business rules are only evaluated at the decision point that enforces them, and may only be relevant at that moment. This is true of our example: Declining applicants who are in dispute with the bureau is a business policy applied only when considering an application; once the product is sold it will not be cancelled if the customer later comes into dispute with the bureau. So in this case there is no value in stating a general business constraint separately from a rule that enforces it at the time of application. The rule is simply part of the knowledge required to take a particular decision.

This example is not unusual; most rules either apply only at a single decision point or occur in different versions at different decision points. For this reason my approach is always to define specifically the rules required at each decision point and to define them as production rules in a way that includes both the constraint and the enforcement regime. Again, this is not radical; this is in practice how almost all rules are defined in the business process automation industry.

Business knowledge formulated in this decision-centric way will be less flexible than if it were expressed as abstract business constraints. For example, it will not be possible to query the rules in multiple ways; they are only capable of making the single decision they are defined for. But it will be considerably simpler. The logic and ontology required to support generic business policy constraints is very sophisticated indeed; for example, one regime is defined by the Object Management Group as the standard SBVR (Semantics of Business Vocabulary and Business Rules), which runs to 422 pages.[7] Specific decision rules will be easier to implement, more efficient to execute, and, I suspect, easier for the business to verbalize.

This is not to say there is no merit in generalizing and reusing rules. Our example rule might be checked at two decision points during the business process, especially if a substantial amount of time elapses between them (for example, if a customer first gets an offer in principle, then comes back a month later for a final quotation). If so it should be included in a common rule set that is encapsulated in both decision services and expressed using a common object model. This common rule set could make a generic decision such as "Is the application eligible?" which would be used by other rules to determine the routing at each decision point. This provides a degree of distinction between policy and enforcement. I also note that even in the worked example for SBVR of a car rental company ("EU-Rent"),[8] rules are grouped into sets that apply at different times, and there are rules that contain expressions such as "at the actual pickup date/time" and "at the transfer drop-off date/time" that effectively tie the rules to particular decision points. So, as we observed at the end of Chapter 2, perhaps the two approaches are not so far apart as it might at first appear.

ALGORITHMS

The humble algorithm is often ignored in discussions about decision management, because it is not an exciting new technology like business rules or predictive analytics. Nevertheless it must be included in this summary of technologies used to encapsulate knowledge, because almost every decision service will also involve some algorithms, and some decision services will involve a *lot*.

An algorithm consists of a sequence of instructions for calculating some result. It is often defined as pseudocode (an informal but structured language that approximates a nonspecific programming language), but can also be represented graphically using flowcharts. In either case the fundamental components are the same: instructions that carry out operations such as input, calculations, and output, and structures that control the flow around the operations, such as "if . . . then . . . else" and "loop until" statements and calls to subprocedures.

One of the principal attractions of business rules is that they are declarative, which means, among other things, that they can be defined without any consideration of order: the decision made by a rule set need not depend on the order of the rules within it. But some business knowledge specifically concerns order in that it specifies operations that must be carried out in a particular sequence. This is particularly true for calculations. Business decisions often involve a substantial number of financial calculations and very often there is no better way to represent these than as a procedure or algorithm. Let's consider three levels of complexity:

1. *Simple expression.* Many financial measures used in decision-making are calculated as ratios, for example, loan-to-value. This ratio can be calculated in a single simple expression:

$$LTV = \frac{\text{Amount of loan}}{\text{Value of security}} \times 100$$

   It could therefore reasonably be captured in a single declarative rule.

2. *Complex expression.* More commonly, the calculation of a measure requires the combination of several or many items of data. For example, disposable income will require the total income to be calculated from all known sources of income, the total expenditure to be calculated from all known expenses, the total expenditure to be subtracted from the total income, and the result multiplied by some weighting. This is probably more logic than you would want to be contained in a single rule, although it could be broken down into a number of rules because the order of the component calculations is not important—only their interrelationship is.

3. *No expression.* Some measures cannot be defined as an expression at all (that is, cannot be simplified to an equation with the measure on its own

on the left-hand side) but can only be calculated from a complex equation using successive approximation, which is inherently procedural. A good example is effective annual percentage rate (EAR or APR).

The legislative definition of APR differs in detail between jurisdictions, but the common principle is that this measure is the hypothetical interest rate that would result in the present value of all the advances made by the lender being equal to the present value of all the payments (fees and repayments) made by the borrower. In other words, it wraps up all the advances and charges made by the lender into a single equivalent rate.

In the European Union the method of calculating APR has been standardized in a directive,[9] and is based on the following equation: "expressing the equivalence of loans on the one hand and repayments and charges on the other." (It is not necessary that you understand this equation!)

$$\sum_{K=1}^{K=m} \frac{A_K}{(1+i)^{t_K}} = \sum_{K'=1}^{K'=m'} \frac{A'_{K'}}{(1+i)^{t_{K'}}}$$

where:

K is the number of a loan.

K' is the number of a repayment or a payment of charges.

A_K is the amount of loan number K.

$A'_{K'}$ is the amount of repayment number K'.

Σ represents a sum.

m is the number of the last loan.

m' is the number of the last repayment or a payment of charges.

t_K is the interval, expressed in years and fractions of a year between the date of loan No. 1 and those of subsequent loans Nos. 2 to m.

$t_{K'}$ is the interval, expressed in years and fractions of a year between the date of loan No. 1 and those of repayments or payments of charges Nos. 1 to m'.

i is the percentage rate that can be calculated (either by algebra, by successive approximations, or by a computer program) where the other terms in the equation are known from the contract or otherwise.

In general, a solution to this equation can only be found by a successive approximation procedure. Start by guessing a value for i, calculate the two sides of the equation using the schedule of loans and payments in the contract, and see whether they are sufficiently close to be considered equal. If they are not (which is quite likely on your first attempt), adjust the value of i in the appropriate direction and recalculate. Keep trying until you find a value of *i* that satisfies the equation. That is the APR.

In some BRMS it would be possible to express this logic as a set of recursive rules, but it wouldn't be pretty. It is much more natural for an analyst to express successive approximation as a procedure. And this is how the U.K. Office of Fair Trading chooses to explain how businesses should conform to the European legislation; in its pamphlet on Credit Charges and APR[10] it provides this algorithm for finding i through successive approximation, using the Bisection Method:

```
; The Bisection Method
begin
        procedure obtain the amounts and times of the advances
        procedure obtain the amounts and times of the installments
        ; set minimum and maximum values for the range of i
        minimum_i=0
        maximum_i=1000
        repeat
        ; calculate i as the midpoint of the current range
        i = minimum_i + (maximum_i - minimum_i) / 2
        procedure calculate 'total_PVs_for_advances'
        procedure calculate 'total_PVs_for_installments'
        ; find which end of the range to move to i
        if total_PVs_for_installments > total_PVs_for_advances
        then minimum_i = i
        else maximum_i = i
        end if
        until maximum_i - minimum_i < 0.0000001
        ; convert the result to a percentage
        print "APR ="; 100 * i
        end
```

In general, one of the most important considerations when deciding whether to use business rules or algorithms is simply this: Which of the two is most natural for the subject matter experts as a medium to express their knowledge?

> **Algorithms**
>
> An *algorithm* is a sequence of instructions for determining some result. Algorithms are typically used for representing decision-making that is inherently *procedural*.
>
> Algorithms are often defined using *pseudocode*: an informal structured language resembling a simple programming language. ■

 PREDICTIVE ANALYTICS

You might think that business rules and algorithms would give you the best possible statement of the business logic for a decision, since they are hand-crafted by people who are experts in the decision-making. This was the mantra in the early days of expert systems, when the sales line was that all the company's decisions should be as good as those made by its foremost expert. But it ain't necessarily so, because there are many things that experts do not know and *cannot* know. Tom Davenport opens his book *Analytics at Work* with these observations:

> If we want to make better decisions and take the right actions, we have to use analytics. Putting analytics to work is about improving performance in key business domains using data and analysis. For too long, managers have relied on their intuition or their "golden gut" to make decisions. For too long, important calls have been based not on data, but on the experience and unaided judgment of the decision maker. Our research suggests that 40 percent of major decisions are based not on facts, but on the manager's gut.[11]

Human knowledge is sometimes unreliable for two reasons:

1. It is based on a single individual's experience, which may not be typical of the business as a whole.
2. Human memory is not perfect and human judgment is subject to a number of well-known cognitive biases.[12]

Predictive analytics is about generating *artificial* business knowledge, which is not subject to these problems, to replace or augment *human* business knowledge. It does this by analyzing historical data, recording what actually happened in a representative set of cases, and using the analysis to create models that will predict objectively what will happen in similar cases in the future.

Analytics is a vast and complex field. Much of it is concerned with providing insights to executives to support their decision-making. As discussed in Chapter, 1 this is the field of business intelligence, which is not covered in this book. This section introduces the principal techniques used to create models that can be deployed in decision services for operational decision-making. As with business rules, it is not possible to provide more than a very brief introduction here. Useful texts are *The Deciding Factor* by Larry Rosenberger, John Nash, and Ann Graham,[13] and *Analytics at Work* by Tom Davenport, Jeanne Harris, and Robert Morison.[14]

Predictive Analytics

Predictive analytics is a set of techniques for generating artificial business knowledge from data recording what happened in a set of historical cases.

The knowledge generated is in the form of *analytic models* that predict what will happen in similar cases in the future. Analytic modeling techniques include *induction, scorecards,* and *neural networks.* ▪

Rule and Tree Induction

Induction is a form of reasoning that makes generalizations from particular observations in order to arrive at a set of general rules. The term is used in contrast to *deduction,* which is the opposite process: logically deriving particular truths from general rules. Induction can be used to generate rules and decision trees automatically from case data.

A rule set that makes a single logical decision can be generated using a process called inductive logic programming (ILP), a term coined by Stephen Muggleton.[15] To use ILP, you must first create two sets of cases: a set of positive examples and a set of negative examples (for example, a set of cases that should be declined and a set of cases that should not be declined). The ILP system interprets these data as facts, and uses logical induction and generalization to generate a set of rules that is consistent with the facts. When applied to a new case, the induced rule set will decide whether the case should be declined.

ILP guarantees to produce a working rule set when the facts provided are complete (they cover the full range of cases to be processed by the induced rule set), and consistent (the decisions are not contradictory on similar cases). This is achievable for coherent, logical domains such as business policy, regulations, and legislation, and these are the areas where ILP tends to be applied. It is very rare, however, for these conditions to be met where the decision concerns human behavior (for example, predicting whether the customer will default on a loan), because human behavior is inconsistent. It is very likely that there are two similar customers in the database, one who defaulted and another who did not. Current research is developing ways of combining ILP with probabilistic reasoning to allow more natural induction of the form "IF x and y THEN PROBABLY z," which could handle behavioral data and be truly predictive. But at present the technologies most commonly used with such data are decision tree learning and scorecards.

Decision trees can be learned from a database of historical cases. Each case is described by a number of input variables and one target variable, which is the value we want the tree to predict. For example, if we had a customer database recording the age, gender, occupation, and income of each customer (the inputs), and what product they actually bought (the target), we could create a tree that, given the same set of inputs for a prospective customer, would predict which product would be of interest to them.

The learning process is recursive. Start with the full set of cases, and find the test, based on a single input variable, which best splits the set into two subsets such that the values of the target variable are as similar as possible *within* each subset but as different as possible *between* the subsets. This test becomes the first node in the tree. Then repeat the process for each of the two subsets you have just created, adding further nodes to the tree. Continue to split the subsets with tests until all the cases in each subset have the same value of the target variable or until no further test will improve the result. These are the leaf nodes.

There are a number of different approaches, based on different definitions of what constitutes the best split. One important approach is ID3, developed by Ross Quinlan,[16] and its subsequent versions C4.5[17] and C5.0. This uses a measure of entropy to identify the test that provides the most information gain.

Once learned, the resulting tree can be represented as a set of rules (as described earlier) and executed in a BRMS.

Scorecards

Rosenberger and Nash quote their FICO colleague Mort Schwartz as saying:

> If an individual credit officer makes three loans to lion tamers that all go bad, that credit officer will probably not lend to lion tamers again. However, the lending organization's experience with *hundreds or thousands* of lion tamers (instead of only three) may be quite different. Human minds organize such qualitative feedback to improve their decision making. The beauty of credit scoring—and computer-based analytic tools like it—is that an entire organization can accumulate and process the experience from vast amounts of data to make quantitative objective decisions on an enterprise level.[18]

Personally I think it quite unlikely that a lending organization would have experience of thousands of lion tamers, but the point is still a good one.

A scorecard is a mathematical model that provides a prediction of the likelihood of a particular event in the form of a numerical score. For example, a credit risk score predicts the likelihood that the customer will default on a loan; a fraud score predicts the likelihood that an application is fraudulent; a bankruptcy score predicts the likelihood that an individual will file for bankruptcy within a certain time. Credit scoring was pioneered in the 1960s by Bill Fair and Earl Isaac, the founders of Fair Isaac Corporation (now FICO).

A scorecard must be created using a substantial database containing cases where the event occurred and cases where it did not; the model is built by comparing these two sets of cases. Each case in the database records a number of *characteristics* of the case (for example, the customer's age, gender, occupation, and income), and the eventual *outcome* (for example, loan repaid or defaulted). Statistical techniques are used to check each of the characteristics to see to what extent it can be used to predict the outcome. The most predictive characteristics (typically 10 to 20) are then combined and weighted so that the more predictive characteristics contribute more to the score. Table 3.2 shows an example of a few characteristics from a scorecard.

This example scorecard captures the business knowledge that older applicants are safer than younger ones, females are safer than males, retirees and self-employed people are safer than students and employees, and high earners are safer than low earners. The characteristics in this example are all single, raw data items, but it is common for scorecards to include more complex characteristics derived from combinations of raw data values (for example, a family type characteristic might be derived from the applicant's marital status and number of dependents). Part of the skill of the analytic modeler lies in finding ways of deriving predictive characteristics from raw data; it is this that makes hand-crafted analytic models more predictive than those generated entirely automatically from raw data.

TABLE 3.2   Scorecard Characteristics

Characteristic	Bin	Partial Score
Age in years	18–21	10
	22–31	12
	32–41	14
	42–46	20
	47–56	22
	57+	25
Gender	F	17
	M	15
	unknown	16
Occupation	employed	12
	student	23
	retired	26
	self-employed	33
	other	27
Income	<50,000	14
	50,000–74,999	18
	75,000–94,999	19
	95,000–149,990	21
	150,000–249,990	22
	250,000+	23

To apply this scorecard to a particular case, each characteristic of the case is used to look up the corresponding partial score, then all the partial scores are added together. The total score indicates a ranking of riskiness rather than a probability, with a high score indicating low risk, and is normalized to an arbitrary scale (often centered around 600).

Note that the contribution of each characteristic is independent of all the others. So, for example, being old will always increase your score, regardless of the other characteristics. Scorecards cannot model interaction between variables. What if it happened to be the case that younger men were riskier than older men, but younger women were safer than older women? (This is a purely hypothetical example, of course.) One solution is to have two versions of the scorecard, one for men and one for women. This is called *segmentation*, and it is very common for score models to be segmented to improve their predictive power. Calculating a score is then a three-stage process:

1. Determine the correct segment for the case.
2. Calculate any derived characteristics.
3. Apply the appropriate scorecard.

However, the independence of the characteristics in scorecards means that the knowledge can be easily represented as a set of rules. The first few rules of the scorecard shown in Table 3.2 would be:

- IF age in years >= 18 and age in years <= 21 THEN add 10 to score.
- IF age in years >= 22 and age in years <= 31 THEN add 12 to score.
- IF age in years >= 32 and age in years <= 41 THEN add 14 to score.

The score is initialized to zero, and when all the applicable rules have fired the score will have its correct value. This rule set can be executed in a BRMS. In some BRMS, scorecards are provided as a standard rule set metaphor, alongside decision tables and decision trees.

There are three broad categories of scorecards:

1. *Application scorecards* are based only on the information provided by the customer as part of an application process (for example, the fields on the application form). Application score models tend to be specific to a single line of business, so businesses usually develop in-house scorecards using their own historical customer data.

2. *Behavioral scorecards* are based on long-term observation of how a customer uses a particular account. For example, it might take into account the customer's history of late payments, trends in the balance on the customer's account, and the amounts and nature of purchases made with the customer's credit card.

3. *Credit scorecards* are based on information from an individual's credit file at the credit reference agency. A credit score is essentially a behavioral score but combines information from all of the individual's accounts with all lenders. The credit reference agency sells the scores on demand as a service to businesses.

Businesses sometimes combine multiple categories of scores to achieve a more robust decision strategy: for example, an in-house behavioral score, an in-house application score, and multiple bureau credit scores.

Scorecards

A *scorecard* is a mathematical model that provides a numerical score representing a prediction of the likelihood of an event.

The total score is calculated by adding the *partial scores* contributed by a number of *characteristics*.

Characteristics may be single *raw* data items, or may be *derived* from a number of data.

A scorecard may be represented as a rule set that can be executed in a BRMS.

Application scorecards are based on data provided by the customer as part of the application process.

Behavioral scorecards are based on long-term observation of how a customer uses a particular account.

Credit scorecards are based on information from an individual's credit file at the credit reference agency. ■

Neural Networks

When I emerged from university with a PhD in neural networks, my first naive venture into business was to take out a patent on the ideas in my thesis and try to sell it. One organization that expressed an interest was Ferranti, at the time an important international electronics and computer systems company. However, in 1981 neural networks were a research topic rather than a proven technology, with significant issues to be resolved, and no one in the organization was prepared to make an investment decision. The buck was passed relentlessly up the management chain until I found myself having lunch with Sebastian de Ferranti himself. Having understood the principles in about five minutes, he delivered a typically straightforward verdict. "I can't see anything coming of this in the near future," he said, "it's all far too speculative. But you seem like a bright enough chap, so why don't you just have a job with us." So I did.

Sebastian was right, about neural networks at least, in the sense that it did take some time for the technology to come to fruition. But they are now a well-established and powerful technology, widely used in analytics and many other fields including speech recognition, image processing, and adaptive control. Neural nets come in many forms, but the archetype for predictive analytics is the multilayer perceptron (MLP) shown in Figure 3.2.

The MLP consists of a number of nodes connected together. The nodes are in layers—an input layer, one or more hidden layers, and an output layer—and typically all the nodes in each layer are connected to all the nodes in the next. Each connection has a weighting associated with it. When used for predictive

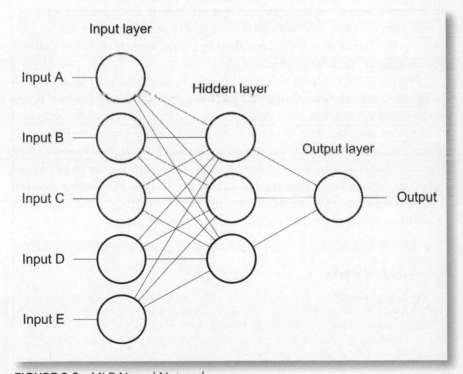

FIGURE 3.2 MLP Neural Network

modeling, each of the inputs would represent a characteristic of the case, and the output would represent a score, just as with a scorecard.

A case is presented to the MLP as a pattern of values applied to the input layer. A wave of activation then passes through the network from the inputs to the outputs. Each node takes each of its inputs from the previous layer, multiplies it by the weighting on that connection, adds all the weighted inputs together, subjects the total to a nonlinear function, and outputs the result to the next layer. The output layer (just one node in Figure 3.1) is the score, which at first is random.

The network can be trained to make useful predictions by repeatedly presenting cases to the inputs and specifying for each one what the correct output should be. A process called back-propagation is used to adjust the weightings.[19] The error is calculated as the difference between the correct output and the actual output, and this is propagated backward through the network, adjusting the weightings according to how much they contributed to the error. Gradually, the weightings adjust themselves until the errors are minimized, that is, until the network produces the correct output for all the input patterns.

The power of neural networks lies in the hidden layers, which allow them to learn very complex nonlinear models that are beyond the capabilities of scorecards. They are often used for fraud modeling, where such complex patterns are common in the behavior to be recognized by the network. However, the phrase "hidden layers" carries a double meaning.

Neural networks have never been very popular with the business community, because the knowledge they learn is kept secret to themselves. When a scorecard is built, any businessperson can inspect the characteristics and understand how the model works. When a neural network has been trained, its knowledge is expressed only as hundreds of numerical weightings and is often incomprehensible even to experienced analysts. So confidence in the model relies entirely on demonstrating that it provides the right predictions through exhaustive testing. As a result, neural networks tend to be used only when other more transparent modeling techniques are not adequate.

Neural Networks

A *neural network* is a simulation of a network of simplified nerve cells. An *MLP* (multilayer perceptron) consists of a number of layers of nodes: an input layer, some hidden layers, and an output layer.

Learning in a neural network is achieved through changes in the *weightings* of the *connections* between the cells.

One method for adjusting the weightings is *back-propagation* of errors. ■

PUTTING IT ALL TOGETHER

Rules, algorithms, and analytic models are not alternative solutions; fully effective knowledge automation requires that they all be used in combination. The three forms of knowledge have different areas of application:

1. *Business rules* are used when there are no historical data available for induction or where knowledge is defined by business policy or legislation. Rules are particularly useful for representing policy that changes frequently (such as marketing strategy), because they are easily updated as required by business experts.
2. *Algorithms* are used for calculations that are inherently procedural. Algorithms tend to be used for business logic that is relatively static (for example, how to calculate the repayments on a loan), because they are less easy to update rapidly.
3. *Predictive analytics* is used where knowledge needs to be acquired empirically, especially to model customer behavior. Analytic models tend to be updated infrequently, because the process involves collecting new behavioral data and building new models.

When to Use Forms of Knowledge

Use *business rules* when no historical data are available to model business policy or legislation, especially if it changes frequently.

Use *algorithms* for calculations that are inherently procedural and do not change frequently.

Use *predictive analytics* to derive knowledge empirically from data, especially to model customer behavior. ▪

Automating decisions in business processes involves four main architectural elements, as shown in Figure 3.3:

1. *DWH.* The data warehouse collects data from BPMS and other sources, such as operational and customer relationship management systems, and makes it available for reporting and analysis.
2. *PAM.* The predictive analytics modeling environment allows the analyst to import, filter, and manipulate samples of customer data; create

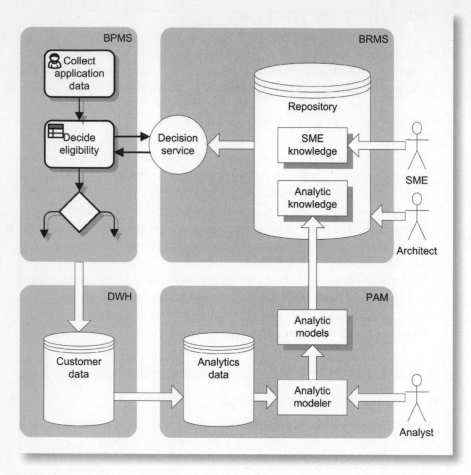

FIGURE 3.3 The Decision Management Cycle

representative sets of cases; and then use those cases to build and test predictive analytic models.

3. *BRMS.* The business rules management system allows the architect to create a repository of business knowledge, including imported analytic models and rules and algorithms provided by subject matter experts, and deploy that knowledge encapsulated in decision services exposed to the BPMS.

4. *BPMS.* The business process management system implements each decision point in its business processes by calling a decision service and using the returned decisions to handle the case. All cases are recorded in the DWH.

Note that these four elements form a cycle. This cycle is a fundamental principle in decision management, because all business knowledge must be constantly tested with real decision-making. The effectiveness of business rules can only be verified by collecting the results of decision-making over a period of time and analyzing the results. (A common approach is "champion-challenger," where two or more alternative sets of rules are applied at random to different cases and the results compared statistically.) Predictive analytic models must also be refreshed periodically because they model customers' behavior, which changes along with the customers' economic and cultural environment.

Architecture for Decision Management

The *DWH* (data warehouse) collects and stores data from BPMS and other sources.

The *PAM* (predictive analytics modeling) environment allows the analyst to build and test predictive analytic models.

The *BRMS* stores business knowledge, including analytic models, and allows it to be deployed in decision services exposed to the BPMS.

The *BPMS* implements each decision point in its business processes by calling a decision service. ■

This cycle may sometimes be difficult to initiate because at the outset the organization may lack the historical data required for model building. However, there are ways around this obstacle. For example, business policy may at first be formulated as a set of business rules and gradually be replaced by analytic models as data are accumulated. Or business rules may have conditions based on weightings or scores whose values are initially based on the judgment of subject matter experts and later derived by predictive analytics.

I first used this approach in 1996, when designing the first rule-based system ever used by the U.K. Inland Revenue, which was for evaluating self-assessment tax returns. Because this was a relatively new form of taxation in the United Kingdom, the Inland Revenue did not have a substantial quantity of historical data for analytic modeling. Instead, I worked with a team of senior tax inspectors over a period of several months to define a set of about 500 rule-based characteristics, which they considered likely to be predictive based on their expertise and experience. The weightings attached to these characteristics were initially based largely on the inspectors' judgment. In parallel, the Inland Revenue started a data mining initiative that would gradually tune these weightings year on year as the data accumulated. Nevertheless, the initial judgments proved to be astonishingly predictive. On our first run, we passed all the U.K. self-assessment taxpayers through the service in a single batch (it took a whole day). When the results were sorted, one of the inspectors pointed to the name at the very top of the list and said, "I know that guy. I've had my eye on him for some time."

Although Figure 3.3 shows the basic architectural components required for decision management, this book is not about architecture; it is about how to run successful knowledge automation projects. The first crucial step in any project is determining the requirements, but the requirements for any knowledge automation project are extremely complex, possibly encompassing many decision services composed of dozens of knowledge components, including hundreds or even thousands of business rules, some to be collected from human experts, others manufactured by analytics. How can we scope, estimate, and plan such a project? A clue to a successful approach is given by the direction of the arrows in Figure 3.3:

- The business processes require decision services.
- The decision services require business knowledge.
- The business knowledge requires analytics.
- The analytics requires data.

    And, because this is a cycle, after all:

- Data collection requires a business process.

But we have to start somewhere. My approach is to start with the business processes and identify the requirements for decision services. I have already addressed the business process context in Chapter 2. This chapter looked ahead to the types of knowledge that will need to be included in the decision services. In Chapter 4, I will describe Decision Requirements Analysis (DRA): a formal, top-down method for identifying the structure of the decision-making to be carried out by decision services, and the knowledge and data required for those decisions. In Chapter 5, I will show how the results of DRA can be used to scope, estimate, plan, and manage a successful knowledge automation project.

 NOTES

1. R. G. Ross, *Principles of Business Rule Approach* (Boston: Addison-Wesley Professional, 2003).

2. B. Von Halle, *Business Rules Applied: Building Better Systems Using the Business Rule Approach* (New York: John Wiley & Sons, 2001).
3. I. Graham, *Business Rules Management and Service Oriented Architecture: A Pattern Language* (Chichester, UK: John Wiley & Sons, 2006).
4. C. L. Forgy, "RETE: A Fast Algorithm for the Many Pattern/Many Object Pattern Matching Problem," *Artificial Intelligence* 19 (1982): 17–37.
5. R. G. Ross, ed., *Business Rules Manifesto: The Principles of Rule Independence.* Version 2.0, Nov. 1, 2003. www.businessrulesgroup.org/brmanifesto.htm.
6. www.businessrulesgroup.org/defnbrg.shtml.
7. OMG. 2008. *Semantics of Business Vocabulary and Business Rules (SBVR),* 1.0. www.omg.org/spec/SBVR/1.0/PDF.
8. *Id.*
9. European Parliament and Council of the European Union. "Directive 98/7/EC of the European Parliament and of the Council of 16 February 1998 amending Directive 87/102/EEC for the approximation of the laws, regulations and administrative provisions of the Member States concerning consumer credit." *Official Journal of the European Communities,* L 101/17 (April 1, 1998).
10. Office of Fair Trading. *Credit Charges and APR: How to Calculate the Total Charge for Credit and the Annual Percentage Rate of Charge* (OFT144), 2007.
11. T. A. Davenport, J. G. Harris, and R. Morison, *Analytics at Work: Smarter Decisions, Better Results* (Boston: Harvard Business School, 2010). Citing Accenture survey of 254 U.S. managers; "Most Companies Say Business Analytics Still Future Goal, Not Present Reality," Accenture press release, December 11, 2008, http://newsroom.accenture.com/article_display.cfm?article_id=4777.
12. T. Gilovich, D. W. Griffin, and D. Kahneman, *Heuristics and Biases: The Psychology of Intuitive Judgment.* (New York: Cambridge University Press, 2002).
13. L. Rosenberger and J. Nash, *The Deciding Factor: The Power of Analytics to Make Every Decision a Winner* (San Francisco: Jossey-Bass, 2009).
14. Davenport, Harris, and Morison, *Analytics at Work.*
15. S. Muggleton, "Inductive Logic Programming," *New Generation Computing* 8, no. 4 (1991): 295–318.
16. J. R. Quinlan, "Induction of Decision Trees," *Machine Learning* 1, no. 1 (1986): 81–106.
17. J. R. Quinlan, *C4.5: Programs for Machine Learning* (San Francisco: Morgan Kaufmann Publishers, 1993).
18. Rosenberger and Nash, *The Deciding Factor.*
19. D. E. Rumelhart, G. E. Hinton, and R. J. Williams, "Learning Internal Representations by Error Propagation," in David E. Rumelhart, James L. McClelland, and the PDP research group (eds.), *Parallel Distributed Processing: Explorations in the Microstructure of Cognition,* 1: *Foundations.* (Cambridge, MA: MIT Press, 1986).

4

Decision Requirements Analysis

HAVE BEEN BUILDING knowledge-based systems now for 30 years, and in my experience the most difficult problems with such projects are rarely technical ones—those are easy to solve. They are the ones that involve management and communication. For example:

- How can you discuss the required decision-making at a high level with all concerned?
- How can you define the scope clearly at the outset of the project before any rules have been collected?
- How can you implement the project in stages without the need for extensive rework?
- How can you avoid nasty surprises halfway through (such as the need to integrate with an extra source of data)?
- How can you divide the development tasks between multiple teams or locations and be sure the components will integrate properly?
- How do you know when you've finished?

Decision Requirements Analysis (DRA) is the approach I have developed as a response to these problems. It is a formal method comprising:

- The Decision Requirements Diagram (DRD): a diagram showing the structure of the required decision-making as a network of decisions and subdecisions with their supporting areas of business knowledge and data
- Decision Requirements Analysis Workshop (DRAW): a structured workshop technique allowing a methodical top-down analysis of a decision into the structure recorded in the DRD and supporting documents
- Best practice guidelines on the use of DRA in project planning, rules discovery, functional design, and system development

The use of DRA in project management will be covered in Chapter 5. In this chapter I will describe the DRD and DRAW, and will start by declaring some initial tenets.

PRINCIPLES

The principles underpinning DRA are simple:

1. *Deliver the requirement and nothing but the requirement.* The success of any implementation project depends on being able to contain the scope and deliver the agreed requirement. The basic principles of sound project management are well understood across the information technology (IT) industry. Unfortunately, business rules projects are notorious for scope creep, often caused by vague requirements and the lack of a clear end goal.

   We must not allow rules projects to be treated as an exception just because they are difficult. Where the business logic to be implemented is very complex, it is even more important that the functional requirement is clearly stated and agreed to by the client. This is not incompatible with iterative development, as I will show. Misunderstandings over scope at the outset of a project can be catastrophic for both supplier and client.

2. *Always work top-down, not bottom-up.* There is a tendency to think that business rules can be randomly harvested from an organization and then assembled into useful repositories. There are many problems with this approach, chiefly:

   - An organization may have millions of business rules, and only a small fraction of them will ever need to be represented in a decision service.
   - A single logical fact may need to be expressed as several different rules for use in different decision-making contexts.

Besides, just collecting and modeling *existing* business rules is anthropology, not decision management. Our goal is to *change* decision-making in the organization, and the only viable approach is top-down: define the desired business decisions, then design and develop the decision services to implement them.

3. *Decision services make decisions.* This may seem too obvious to state, but it is surprising how often this basic truth is ignored. A decision service is fundamentally a decision-making component. So, although it could be specified in various ways (for example, as a function, an object, or an input-output mapping), the best way to define its functionality is purely in terms of the decisions it makes. Each decision can be defined as a means of providing an answer to a question. So if you can clearly define the questions, the answers, and the means, you have completely defined the functionality of the rule service.

4. *Decisions require information.* You can discover the requirements of a decision by asking *what information is required* to make the decision. Information is of three kinds:

    1. Business knowledge (in all its forms: business rules and their metaphors, algorithms, and analytic models)
    2. Data describing the case to be decided on
    3. The results of other decisions

    The last point is the key: Decisions depend on subdecisions. This allows decision-making to be decomposed into a network that can be drawn in a Decision Requirements Diagram (DRD).

The Principles of Decision Requirements Analysis

1. Deliver the requirement and nothing but the requirement.
2. Always work top-down, not bottom-up.
3. Decision services make decisions.
4. Decisions require information. ■

 ## DECISION REQUIREMENTS DIAGRAM

People are *much* better at extracting information from pictures than from words, which is why diagrams are used in every professional sphere. IT is especially blessed with diagrams; Unified Modeling Language (UML) 2.3 alone provides 14 different types.[1]

Unfortunately, I have found none of these to be much use for defining requirements for decision-making. Use case diagrams are intended for use in requirements definition, but they treat the system as a black box rather than exposing the structure of its decision-making. Entity relationship diagrams can be used for capturing knowledge structure (as Barb von Halle and Larry Goldberg have elegantly shown in their Decision Model[2]) but are more useful for modeling specific rules than high-level requirements.

This section will describe the Decision Requirements Diagram (DRD), which is used for capturing the scope and structure of the required decision-making at the very outset of a rules project before any rules are discovered. This diagram, with its associated documentation, is central to the DRA method.

Definition

A DRD is a network diagram that shows the information required for one or more decisions. Technically speaking, it is a directed acyclic graph, that is, it consists of a number of nodes connected by unidirectional arrows and contains no loops. It can be thought of as a decomposition of some decision-making into a set of interrelated decisions and areas of supporting information. Figure 4.1 shows a simple example of a DRD for a decision on how to deal with an application for a secured loan. This example is unrealistically simple for a real application, but shows all the principal features of a DRD.

The DRD contains three types of nodes: decisions, knowledge, and data. These are linked by arrows that indicate requirements: an arrow from A to B indicates that A is required for B. So, for example, the decision "Risk acceptable" requires three pieces of information: the result of the decision "Application risk score," business knowledge expressed as tables, and bureau data. By convention, the nodes are arranged so that the arrows point upward. Note that the diagram is not necessarily a tree: A single piece of information (for example, the application risk score or the requested loan data) may be required by multiple decisions.

The DRD contains only decision nodes, knowledge nodes, data nodes, and arrows.

Decision nodes represent the decisions that are required to be made. These may be made by a decision service, but not necessarily; they might alternatively be made by a human decision maker or by some other system component. The allocation of decisions to decision-making agents will be carried out after the decision requirements are established.

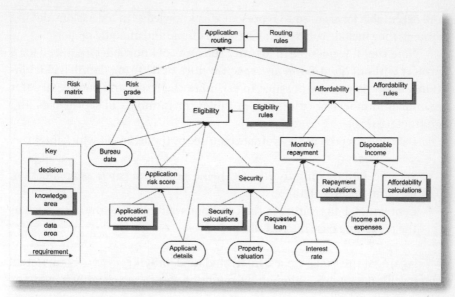

FIGURE 4.1 A Simple DRD

Each decision generates a set of results (decision values), using a set of inputs (data areas and the results of other decisions). The detailed business logic used to implement the decision is described in one or more knowledge nodes; the decision node applies that knowledge to the inputs to derive the results.

Decision nodes are described in increasing detail as the project progresses. The initial colloquial description will include:

- *Name*: a short noun phrase used as a label for the decision (for example, "Risk grade").
- *Question and answer*: a natural language question characterizing the decision (such as, "What category of risk is presented by this application?") with a defined set of answers (such as, {RG1, RG2, RG3, RG4, RG5}).
- *Description*: a brief definition of the decision-making logic or process (for example "Risk grade is obtained from the risk matrix using the bureau credit score and application score").

Knowledge nodes represent areas of business knowledge required for the decisions. This knowledge may currently exist as human expertise, printed documents, and so on, or it may not exist yet. Chapter 3 described some of the executable forms used to represent this knowledge in a decision-making system; they include rule sets, tables, algorithms, and analytic models.

Note that it is possible to identify the *areas* of knowledge required for a project without identifying any specific rules or defining detailed calculations, and it is usually possible to estimate their size and complexity (for example, numbers of rules, size of tables, or numbers of scorecards and characteristics).

Data nodes represent areas of data required by the decisions, which might be:

■ Specific data relating to the case being processed (such as application, account, or claim data).
■ Contextual data relating to the conditions surrounding the case (such as the prevailing base interest rate).

Again, at this stage we are interested in identifying *areas* of data, not all the specific data items, although we might be able to say roughly how many items were involved.

Arrows represent requirements: the fact that a piece of information is used by a decision. Requirements are not conditional; the arrow must be present if the piece of information is *ever* required to make the decision.

The Decision Requirements Diagram

A *DRD* (Decision Requirements Diagram) is a network diagram that shows the information required for one or more decisions.

A DRD contains decision nodes, knowledge nodes, and data nodes, connected by arrows.

Decision nodes represent the decisions that are required to be made.

Knowledge nodes represent areas of business knowledge required for the decisions.

Data nodes represent areas of data required by the decisions.

Arrows represent the dependency of a decision on a piece of information. ■

Uses

The main uses of the DRD are described in detail in Chapter 5, but here is a teaser.

The definitions of the nodes are directly useful in themselves:

- The decision nodes provide a clear but succinct definition of the functional requirements for decision-making.
- The knowledge nodes identify all the areas of knowledge to be captured or modeled during the project.
- The data nodes identify all the areas of data to be made available to decision services and modeled within them.

The arrows between the nodes have important implications for the design, including:

- Data flow: If the source of some information is external to the system component in which the decision is to be implemented, a data interface is required.
- Ordering of tasks: If decision B requires the result of decision A, A must be evaluated before B.

Drawing a boundary around a subset of nodes allows a very clear definition of what is inside and what is outside the boundary, and the lines crossing the boundary indicate the interfaces necessary. This allows:

- Project scoping: by drawing a boundary around all the nodes to be implemented in the project
- Allocation of functionality to systems: by drawing boundaries between a number of decision services and/or other system components
- Iterative development: by partitioning nodes between a number of increments
- Project resource allocation: by allocating nodes to teams or individuals

Figure 4.2 shows how a boundary drawn on the DRD may be used to define the scope of a project. This example shows a fairly common scenario: all the decision and knowledge nodes are inside the boundary (that is, decision services must implement all the defined decision-making) and all the data nodes are outside (that is, all the required data must be provided by the client infrastructure to the decision services).

Figure 4.3 shows how the DRD may be used to define project increments for iterative design and development, for example, in projects managed using the Rational Unified Process (RUP). In this example, the decisions and knowledge nodes are divided into three increments, each providing a distinct functional benefit. Decision Requirements Analysis has allowed this division to be planned so that the three increments are loosely coupled, that is, connected by few arrows.

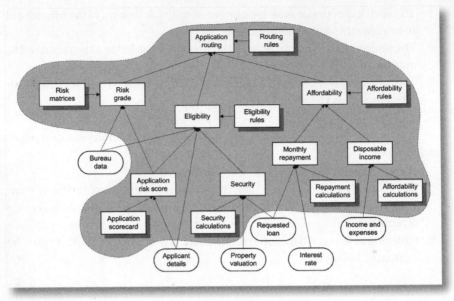

FIGURE 4.2   Project Scope Boundary on the DRD

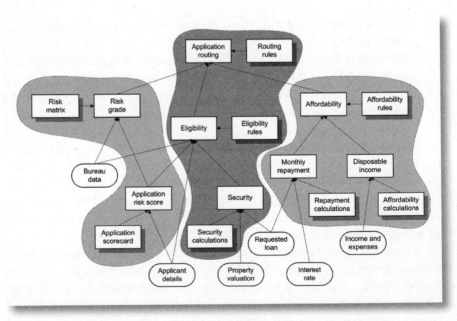

FIGURE 4.3   Project Increments on the DRD

As simple as they are, these diagrams are staggeringly useful, because they allow the broad scope and structure of the decision-making to be appreciated at a glance and discussed by all the people involved in the project: the project sponsors, project managers, business domain experts, analysts, designers, developers, and testers. They allow people to point to things and say "*this* component of the decision-making," without having to refer to anything technical or architectural.

The DRD is produced using a simple, structured workshop technique called DRAW.

 ## DRAW

DRAW is a structured workshop technique for defining the decision-making requirements for a set of decision services and documenting them using DRDs. There are two typical contexts for DRAW:

1. It can be carried out as a self-contained activity to establish the resources required for a potential knowledge automation project (for example, to establish feasibility, to prioritize alternative projects, or to produce a road map for multiple deliveries).
2. It can be carried out in the first few days of an implementation project to define the requirements for decision-making (as a requirements task in waterfall or an inception task in RUP).

The requirements established in the DRAW sessions will usually be recorded in a document including one or more DRDs.

Resources

No special facilities are required by way of accommodation or software. The workshops can be held in any quiet meeting room with a flip chart, whiteboard, and projector. Interaction is improved if the participants sit around a table rather than all sitting facing the analyst as in a presentation. If no specific editing tool is available, the DRD can be sketched on the whiteboard during the workshops and drawn out formally later using any commonly available diagram editor.

The success of DRAW is entirely dependent on the caliber and commitment of the people involved, so it is important that the right team is assembled for the workshops. The following should be present full-time:

- *Decision analyst*: facilitates the workshops, analyzes the results, and records the agreed upon requirements in one or more DRDs and their supporting documentation
- *Scribe*: supports the decision analyst by keeping notes of agreements reached in the workshop, requests for further information, outstanding actions, and so on
- *Business domain experts*: contribute subject-matter expertise, represent business process users, help to foster user acceptance and involvement
- *Business analysts*: responsible for the business process redesign and the definition of the functional requirements for business process automation

This core team should be supported part-time by:

- *Project sponsors*: ultimately responsible for defining the goals and success criteria for the project
- *Project managers*: responsible for project planning, day-to-day project management, liaising and reporting, and providing resources
- *Decision service architect*: will be responsible for the design of the decision services to implement the agreed upon requirements.
- *Technical architects*: provide background on the technical context for the implementation (for example, overall systems architecture, general IT requirements or standards, available data sources and interfaces, legacy systems to be replaced)

The decision analyst will lead the workshops, conduct the analysis, and produce the outputs. Most of the input will come from the domain experts and the business analysts. The technical architects should ideally be on call throughout, but must attend any meetings concerning data sources and interfaces. The project sponsors and managers should be present for the initial kick-off and for any final decisions on project scope.

Scheduling

DRAW works best in small groups (6 to 12 knowledgeable people) rather than large workshops. You should start with one or more plenary workshops to draw out the top-level requirements, then pursue more detailed analyses with subgroups or individual specialists as necessary. It is not necessary to explore the whole network with each person; individual areas of expertise or responsibility may correspond to different regions of the network. It is, however, a good idea to cross-check results with multiple staff. Individuals will miss items and there may be differences of opinion that reveal important business issues that need to be clarified. After the results have been analyzed and documented, the draft DRDs should be presented at a final plenary session for general agreement.

Although it is possible to carry out a very high-level DRAW in a single day, it is more typical for it to require a number of workshops over several days. A good approach for a typical project involving a single business process is to set aside a week, leaving two or three half days empty for overruns or follow-up work. This will often be more convenient for business domain experts who have other demands on their time.

Be flexible. It is useful to have a prearranged agenda but it is unlikely you will be able to follow it exactly, as it is impossible to predict which areas of the decision-making will require most discussion. As the network is revealed you may also find it useful to contact and interview additional people. However, it is very useful to have a good idea of the scale of the engagement in advance. I once arrived in Johannesburg, South Africa, expecting to run a short DRAW session with half a dozen experts, covering an extension to the existing originations process for a single retail credit product. I found 40 people in a huge room wanting a full enterprise-wide process redesign covering all the company's product portfolio. That's probably taking flexibility too far. Luckily, I love working with South Africans.

The Method

In principle, DRAW consists of a standard sequence of five stages:

1. Identify the decision points.
2. Define the top-level decisions.
3. Decompose the decision-making.
4. Describe all the nodes in detail.
5. Define the decision service boundaries.

These are described in the following sections. Of course, few real workshops will run quite this smoothly; things will emerge that require you to backtrack and

The Five Stages of DRAW

1. Identify the decision points in the business process.
2. Define the top-level decisions for each decision point.
3. Decompose the decision-making for each top-level decision.
4. Describe all the decision, knowledge, and data nodes in detail.
5. Define the decision service boundaries. ■

modify or add detail to the results of previous stages. This is not a problem, so long as the basic principles are followed and the eventual outputs are sound and complete.

Stage 1: Identify the Decision Points

Start by discussing the business process and what the organization hopes to achieve from this project. Try to understand the drivers: What transformations do the sponsors intend to bring about in their business? What benefit do they hope to achieve through decision management?

Investigate in detail all the points in the business process where automated decisions will be required of decision services; these are the decision points. Give each decision point a name and define

- The stage in the business process where this decision point occurs.
- The type of decision-making carried out at this stage.
- The intended role of the decision service in the decision-making.
- The role of any users or other system components.

Document the results using some sort of business process flow or workflow diagram. The process needs to be described to a sufficient level of detail such that each decision point is a single atomic task or activity in the flow, involving only the decision service that automates the decision. All interactions with other agents—users and systems—must occur in separate tasks before or after the decision point. This ensures that it will be possible to analyze the data flow requirements: All data used at the decision point must be collected before that point, and the results returned by the decision point can only be used after that point.

Figure 4.4 shows a simple example of what might be on your whiteboard at the end of Stage 1. This process flow, following the conventions of BPMN 2.0, includes two decision points shown as business rule tasks: *Pre-bureau* and *Post-bureau*. These correspond to the *Bureau strategy* and *Application routing* decision points in the originations template (see Figure 2.7). Most real business processes would be more complex than this, but not all. Some would be simpler: for example, a batch process that is triggered monthly and does no more than collect data, call a decision service, and store the results.

Chapter 2 discussed some of the issues surrounding decision automation and showed that introducing automated decision-making may involve redesigning the surrounding business process. As a result, the time required for this stage of DRAW is highly variable. I have worked on projects where the business process was fixed, and the decision points were therefore predefined and could be characterized in a few hours. I have also worked on projects where defining

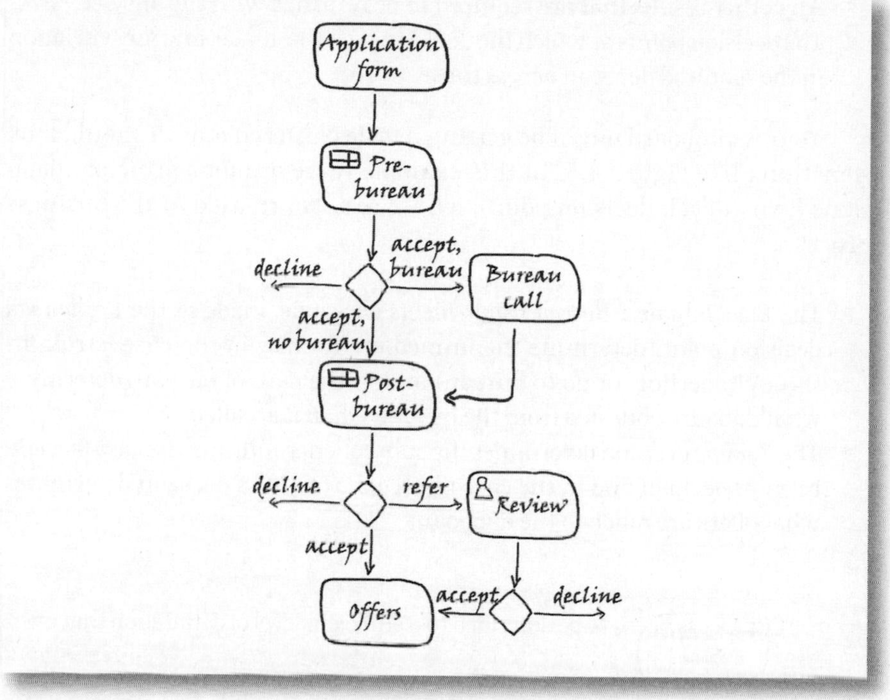

FIGURE 4.1 DRAW Stage 1—Decision Points

the decision points for automation took place as part of a complete process redesign, which took several weeks.

Stage 2: Define the Top-Level Decisions

For each decision point, establish the principal decisions that are required to be made by decision services, expressed in the most general possible terms. By principal I mean the decisions that will actually be used in the process (for example, for routing or case handling). Wherever similar decisions are made at multiple decision points, try to generalize the decisions across those contexts. Even if there are expected to be multiple decision services *do not at this stage attempt to allocate decisions to particular services*, just identify what decisions have to be made.

Give each decision a name, then establish the following:

- A question that characterizes the decision, expressed clearly in natural language with a defined set of answers.

- Any other results that are required to be returned with the answer.
- The decision points at which the decision has to be made, and any variation in the required decision across these.

Your whiteboard might be getting a little cluttered now; it should look something like Figure 4.5. In this example there are four principal decisions (two at each decision point), whose results are used in the business process:

- The *Eligibility* and *Bureau requirements* decisions, made at the *Pre-bureau* decision point, determine the immediate routing of the case (straight-through, decline, or go to bureau) and in the case of bureau, determine what data are obtained from the bureau when it is called.
- The *Routing* decision determines the subsequent routing of the case (accept, refer, or decline) and in the case of accept, the *Offers* decision determines what offers are made to the applicant.

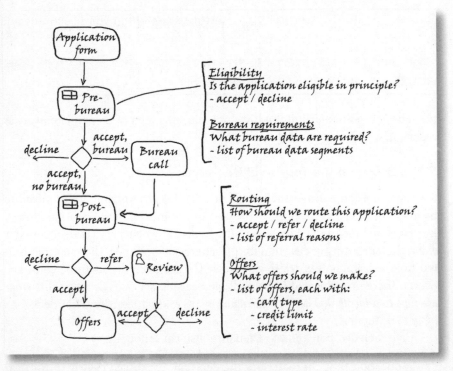

FIGURE 4.5 DRAW Stage 2—Principal Decisions

Stage 3: Decompose the Decision-Making

Now we can build our DRD. Start by drawing the top-level decisions identified in stage 2 on the board as separate, unconnected boxes. In our example these are *Eligibility*, *Bureau requirements*, *Routing*, and *Offers*. Then follow an iterative process. Choose any decision and ask: "What information is required to make this decision?" Fully explore the following possibilities:

- Areas of business knowledge (existing or yet to be created)
- Areas of data (specific data describing the case or contextual data)
- The results of other decisions (subdecisions)

Add knowledge, data, or decision nodes to the DRD as required, and connect them to the decision you are addressing. Each new decision node added to the DRD in this way should be defined like the top-level decisions. It can then be addressed in its turn. Note that because this process is recursive and only analyzes one decision at a time, it is not more difficult to decompose a large decision-making requirement, it just takes longer.

For example, when you ask: "What information do you need to decide whether the application is eligible in principle?" the domain experts might reply, "Well, we have a number of business policies based on application details like age, and not being unemployed, and so on. Oh yes, and one of the policies is a minimum risk score, so we need that, too." This tells you to add a knowledge node for policy rules, a data node for applicant details, and a decision node for a risk score subdecision and link them all to the *Eligibility* decision node.

You can then ask the same question about the risk score: "What information do you need to decide *that?*" The experts tell you they use a scorecard based purely on application data, so you just need to add a knowledge node for the scorecard and link the application data node you have already created to the risk score decision. At this point your DRD will look like Figure 4.6.

There are now no more decisions to be addressed for *Eligibility*, so you can turn your attention to the next principal decision: *Bureau requirements*. You are told, "We buy bureau data for all applicants, unless they've been declined, obviously. We buy a standard set of credit data for everybody, but if their application score is marginal we also buy a credit score. We have a table that says for different types of applicant what band of risk score is considered marginal." This tells you that the *Bureau requirements* decision depends on the *Eligibility* and *Risk score* decisions, uses application data, and involves business knowledge in the form of a table. The DRD now looks like Figure 4.7.

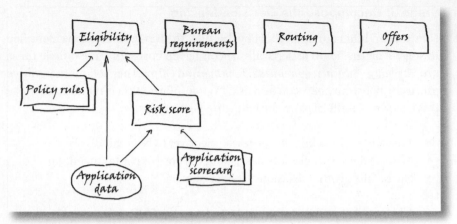

FIGURE 4.6 DRAW Stage 3—DRD

Gradually your DRD will expand to cover the board, and things might get a bit messy (multiple colors help). But when the process is complete you will have a complete DRD, identifying all the decisions required, the areas of knowledge involved in the decisions, and the areas of data required by the decisions. The four separate principal decisions you started with will probably have been joined together, either directly (like *Eligibility* and *Bureau requirements*) or indirectly through shared subdecisions.

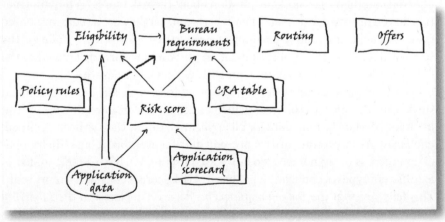

FIGURE 4.7 DRAW Stage 3—DRD Continued

The size of the whiteboard can become a constraint, so it is sometimes more convenient to draw a separate DRD for each decision point. This is fine, so long as you bear in mind that they are, in principle, just one big DRD, and the results of decisions made at one decision point can be used as inputs by a decision in a subsequent decision point. It is important that this is recorded in the second decision point as a dependency between decisions, not as a source of data. Imagine, in our example, that we used separate diagrams for the two decision points, and the *Routing* decision involved rules that referred high-risk cases for review, based on their application risk score. In this situation the *Pre-bureau risk score* decision node should also appear on the post-bureau DRD, linked to the *Routing* decision node. It should then be identified as a connector, rather than duplicating all its dependencies (I just put an asterisk on it).

While conducting this analysis, the decision analyst must constantly make judgments about the level of granularity to seek in decomposing the decision-making. As a rule of thumb, you have reached a complete analysis when you can see how each knowledge area might be implemented as a single type of business knowledge, as discussed in Chapter 3. This is what I meant in my closing remarks in Chapter 2 by an approach of "top-down with look-ahead." The decision analyst does not need to be a designer himself, but needs a basic familiarity with the techniques that are available to the designer. Of course, these depend on the particular features of the BRMS that will be used. If the BRMS has not yet been selected when the DRAW is conducted, the technologies described in Chapter 3 will be a good set to assume.

Stage 4: Describe All the Nodes In Detail

After a coffee break and some fresh air, you should revisit all the nodes in the DRD and discuss them in detail, one by one.

For each decision node, investigate thoroughly how the relevant knowledge and data are used in reaching the decision. Check for any exceptions to the standard scenario that has been described so far. If necessary, agree on a more detailed description that covers all scenarios.

Investigate each knowledge node, and record:

- The source of the knowledge (for example, documents, spreadsheets, personnel, legacy systems, or analytics)
- An estimate of its size and complexity (such as approximate number of rules or pages of calculations)

- Who will be responsible for providing the knowledge (preferably a specific name)
- The maintenance requirements, including who will be updating the knowledge (business or IT staff), and how often
- Any other important background (for example, constraints on availability of the individual designated as the source of the knowledge and any plans to introduce new types of decision-making within the timescale of the project)

Investigate each data node, and record:

- The source of the data (paper form, input screen, web service or database)
- An estimate of its size and complexity (for example, approximate number of data items)
- Who will be responsible for defining the data interface
- Any other important background (for example, the accuracy and completeness of the data source, any possible modifications within the timescale of the project)

This process involves some repetition; going over the requirements collected during Stage 3. This is deliberate: It is an opportunity to check that the information you recorded is correct and complete.

Note that at this stage the objective is not to collect *actual knowledge* (such as particular business rules or algorithms), but just to describe the required *areas* of knowledge and identify their sources for subsequent discovery. However, it is likely that the experts will offer example rules as part of their explanations, and if so, these should be recorded. Similarly, the objective when documenting the data nodes is to identify *areas* of data, not a full object model.

Stage 5: Define the Rule Service Boundaries

Having defined the decision structure and documented all the supporting information, decide which nodes are to be implemented as part of a decision service and which are to remain in external systems. Do not at this stage try to decide how many decision services there should be and how decisions should be allocated between them; this is a design matter and we are involved here with requirements gathering. Simply identify which nodes are to be implemented and which are not. This will provide you with a "scope boundary," as shown in Figure 4.2.

Some useful rules of thumb when agreeing on the scope boundary are:

- The top-level decision nodes will be implemented in decision services (this was our starting assumption).
- Most of the subdecisions and their supporting knowledge nodes will be implemented in decision services, but some may be implemented (perhaps temporarily) in other decision-making processes, such as legacy systems or human authorities. The results of these external decisions should be collected before the decision service is called, and passed into the service as data.
- Most data nodes will be information sources outside the decision services, but some may be implemented for convenience within the services if no other system requires access to them.

Boundary analysis involves provisional architectural decisions, so the boundaries may be subject to change later in the design process. For this reason it is important that all stakeholders attend the final DRAW session, in which the results are presented and the DRD and the scope boundary are agreed on with all present.

Once agreed upon in the final meeting, the results of DRAW can be recorded in a requirements document. They include:

- The business process flows and decision points
- The principal decisions
- The DRD and supporting descriptions of all the nodes
- The scope boundary

This is a lightweight document—perhaps 20 pages long—but once approved it is a *very* precise statement of the scope of the decisions to be automated. What makes this statement of scope so powerful is that it is based on a detailed analysis of the *structure* of the decision-making, not just a vague estimate of its volume. This understanding of decision structure will allow accurate project estimation, robust project planning, a clean design, structured knowledge discovery, efficient

---

Ten Tips for the Decision Analyst

1. **Have a plan.** There are few things more embarrassing than sitting down with a roomful of subject matter experts (SMEs) and having to say, "Well, what are we going to talk about today?" DRAW is a

(Continued)

Ten Tips for the Decision Analyst *(Continued)*

structured process, which helps a lot, but you should go further than this, breaking the domain up by process or line of business. Create and circulate an agenda before the workshops so that the SMEs know what they will be expected to discuss in each session. This will allow them to prepare properly and bring relevant supporting materials.

2. **Explain the process.** To contribute properly, the SMEs need to understand what is happening in the workshops, where they are heading, and what the goals are. Explain the principles and approach of DRAW and describe the intended outputs. It is important that everyone understands the form of the results expected from the workshop and the level of detail required, that is, they will be expected to define exactly what decisions need to be made, but will not be expected to provide any actual business rules.

3. **Take control, keep control.** Insist on following the process, as far as is useful. It is important to be flexible, up to a point, and there will be occasions when it is necessary to take detours, but this must be at your discretion. SMEs are often people with strong personalities, so it can sometimes be a challenge to stop individuals from hijacking the meeting. It is your role to facilitate and control the discussion, not simply to record it, and it is ultimately your responsibility to ensure that the goals of the session are achieved.

4. **Collaborate.** Do not simply document the existing processes and business logic described in the meetings. Your role is to help the organization restructure its processes and decision-making to reap the benefits of decision management, so you need to question, challenge, and make suggestions. If you have experience in other projects or domains this will be valuable: "Have you thought of doing it this way?"

5. **Insist on clarity.** If something doesn't make complete sense to you, either you don't understand it properly or something is wrong or inconsistent. In either case you need to clarify it. Don't be afraid of asking stupid questions: you are the analyst, not the SME, and your ignorance can actually be useful in ensuring a complete specification that exposes all the assumptions that are normally unspoken.

6. **Resolve contradictions.** If you do discover any inconsistencies or disagreements, record these as issues and pass them back to the organization for resolution by escalation if necessary. The decision services can only implement one coherent body of corporate policy; this must be agreed on among all stakeholders.

7. **Double-check everything.** There are all sorts of tricks for asking the same question twice in different words. Check all general rules by

Ten Tips for the Decision Analyst *(Continued)*

asking if there are any exceptions. "Is that always true? So this never happens?" Always ask to confirm your understanding, replaying your interpretation of the requirement back to the SMEs for their confirmation before moving on to the next topic.

8. **Document everything.** There will be many occasions when you think, "That's so obvious I don't need to record it." Then you will find you have forgotten it as soon as you leave the room (this is especially true if you are dealing with several projects at the same time). Record it with whatever tools you are using. If you are using a whiteboard, label it, date it, and take a photograph of it.

9. **Look after yourself.** Running a series of DRAW sessions requires your full concentration over several days and can be taxing. You cannot do this effectively if you are tired or hungover. I speak from shameful experience.

10. **Be yourself, enjoy yourself.** Everyone has his or her own individual style. Consultancy is a form of human interaction and must be based on honesty, so relax, be natural, have a good time, share a joke with the SMEs. This has two advantages: first, it puts the experts at ease, encourages them to discuss issues more openly, and defuses tension; second, you will have more fun. Work should be fun. ■

implementation with reusable code, avoidance of scope creep, and reduced risk of overruns. How this is all achieved is explained in the next chapter.

 NOTES

1. Object Management Group, *OMG Unified Modeling Language (OMG UML), Super-structure Version 2.3* (2010) OMG Document Number: formal/2010-05-05, www.omg.org/spec/UML/2.3/Superstructure.
2. B. Von Halle and L. Goldberg, *The Decision Model: A Business Logic Framework Linking Business and Technology* (Boca Raton, FL: Auerbach Publications, 2010).

CHAPTER FIVE

Using DRA in Knowledge Automation Projects

L ET ME SUMMARIZE OUR PROGRESS SO FAR. We have remodeled our business processes, identifying a set of decision points that will be automated by encapsulating our organization's business knowledge in decision services. We have defined the structure of the decision-making to be implemented at these decision points using Decision Requirements Analysis (DRA). As a result we have a complete set of high-level functional requirements for knowledge automation, expressed as business process flows and Decision Requirements Diagrams (DRDs) with supporting documentation. Now we need to design, implement, and deploy a set of decision services to meet these requirements.

Such projects can be fraught with problems, and many of these problems result from a lack of *structure*. This chapter provides some advice on how these problems can be mitigated, or completely avoided, by using the decision structure revealed in the DRDs as a template to provide a structure for the project, a structure for knowledge discovery, a structure for the design, and a structure for the implementation.

DRA IN PROJECT MANAGEMENT

The decision structure revealed through DRA has several important roles in ensuring a well-managed knowledge automation project:

- It provides a basis for a clear contractual definition of the scope of the project.
- It provides metrics for estimation of effort and timescales.
- It suggests a structure for project and resource planning.
- It allows definition of increments for iterative or agile project management.
- It allows full traceability of project deliverables to the original requirements.

For these reasons DRA was adopted by FICO in 2005 and incorporated into its RUP-based methodology FIRUP (Fair Isaac Rational Unified Process), as a standard tool for decision requirements definition and project management. Since then it has been applied on many different knowledge automation projects around the world with great success.

Automation Scoping

The DRA Workshop (DRAW) is essentially a scoping exercise, and should therefore be carried out as early as possible in a knowledge automation project. (As discussed in Chapter 2, the requirements for decision services should be considered alongside, and as part of, any business process redesign.)

The results of DRAW should be recorded in a document that will define the scope of the decisions to be automated. The precise role of this automation scoping document will depend on the context of the work, the methodology adopted, and the parties involved, for example:

- It might provide an assessment of feasibility and cost in support of the early stages of developing a business case for project funding.
- It might form a contractual document between a client and a supplier, specifying the scope of supply for a subsequent development project.
- It might be a high-level requirements document produced in the first stage of a development project (the requirements phase under waterfall; the inception phase under RUP), to clarify the scope and facilitate project planning.

The earlier DRAW is carried out, the greater will be the benefits of the automation scoping document to the organization. As a requirements document, the results will help greatly in project planning and management, but only within the context of a project whose scope has already been broadly agreed on. If DRAW is carried out as a separate scoping study prior to the development project, the results allow project costing and support negotiation. If used for feasibility assessment, DRAW can evaluate a number of opportunities competing for funding and support a go/no-go decision.

I have used DRAW in all these scenarios. Here are examples from FICO projects I have worked on:

- *For feasibility assessment*: As part of a team providing consultancy to a U.K. health insurer, I helped to review a number of business processes, identifying potential opportunities for automating decision-making, and assessing these using decision yield. I then conducted DRAW sessions on the most promising opportunities. The results were used to decide on feasibility, estimate the costs of development, and produce a road map for implementation.
- *For contractual scoping*: One recent project to automate originations for a U.K. building society was divided into two separate contracts. In the first phase, DRAW was used to define the scope of automation, and the technical architecture was designed. These results were then used to specify a contractual statement of work for the second phase and provide a more accurate estimate of the costs of implementation.
- *For definition of high-level requirements*: A South African furniture retailer engaged FICO to implement a major enterprise-wide process automation project for credit originations. The project began by using DRAW to scope the automation required for each line of business. The results were recorded as functional requirements documents for the decision services to be developed. The Decision Requirements Analysis also allowed the development of a common object model across all lines of business and substantial reuse of decision structures.

Whatever scenario provides the context for DRAW, the form of the resulting document is always essentially the same. Whatever its role, it should contain at least the following sections:

1. Business Context: the background to the project, including the goals of decision automation and the project success criteria.
2. Decision Points: a description of the business process, supported by business process flow diagrams, specifying the points at which decisions are

required of automated services and the principal decisions to be made at those points.

3. Decision Structure: DRD(s) for the required decision points, supported by verbal definitions of all of the nodes, including estimates of size and complexity for knowledge and data nodes.

4. Scope of Automation: a statement of the scope of the decisions to be automated, defined as a set of nodes on the DRD and illustrated with a diagram showing a boundary around those nodes on the DRD, as shown in Figure 4.2.

The Automation Scoping Document

The automation scoping document:

▪ Defines the requirements for a project to automate decision-making.

▪ Can be used for feasibility assessment, for contractual scoping, or as a project requirements document.

▪ Always has the following contents:

1. Business context: project background, goals, and success criteria.

2. Decision points: a specification of the points in the business process at which decision services are called and the principal decisions to be made at those points.

3. Decision structure: DRD(s) for the required decision points, supported by verbal definitions of all of the nodes.

4. *Scope of automation*: a statement of the scope of the decisions to be automated, defined using boundaries drawn on the DRD. ▪

This is a simple, brief document, but provides a very clear definition of the requirements for automated decision-making, allowing the scope to be tightly controlled. This implies that the document must be reviewed and signed off by the project sponsors before any subsequent work is carried out. This is not to prevent changes during the project but to allow them to be properly managed. By basing the definition of project scope on the results of DRAW, any proposals to change the scope boundary can be assessed for their impact on the project.

For example, every single business rule proposed for implementation should help to determine one of the decisions in scope, belong to one of the knowledge areas in scope, and use only data provided by the data areas in scope. If rules are discovered that do not fit into these constraints, the agreed-on change control procedure should be followed to consider the cost of extending the scope to include the new decisions, knowledge areas, or data. This may seem draconian, but it is a very effective check on scope creep, which is a common problem with business rules projects. Provided a thorough Decision Requirements Analysis has been conducted such changes should seldom be required.

Estimation

Once the scope has been agreed on, the process flows, DRD, and scope boundary provide a number of metrics that can be used for estimating the effort that will be required for a project to implement the decision services. These metrics have different significance as indicators:

- The number of *decision points* is an indicator of the number of instances of decision services to be deployed and tested.
- The number of *decision nodes* in scope is an indicator of the number of separate decisions to be implemented and tested and the amount of output data to be modeled and returned from the decision services.
- The number and complexity of the *data nodes* required (i.e., those linked to decision nodes in scope) are indicators of the amount of input data to be modeled and provided to the decision services.
- The number, type, and complexity of the *knowledge nodes* in scope are indicators of the amount of business knowledge to be discovered, implemented, and tested.
- The number of *arrows* linking decision nodes in scope is an indicator of the overall complexity (interconnectedness) of the decision-making.

These indicators can be used to create models that predict project effort. More or less complex models are possible, using different combinations of indicators. For feasibility assessment, a very simple model might be used to provide a ballpark estimate of overall project cost; this could be based purely on the decision points and the knowledge nodes, since these are by far the most important indicators. For detailed project planning, more sophisticated models can be used to predict the effort required for specific project tasks (this will be discussed in the next section).

You should not expect to be able to take one of these models off the shelf. The effort required to automate a given scope will vary with a number of factors specific to your organization, including:

- The project methodology to be used, including documentation standards and testing strategy. Different methodologies impose different levels of overhead and carry different levels of risk.
- The solution architecture, especially the business rules management system (BRMS) chosen, the type of services to be deployed, and the knowledge maintenance facilities to be provided.
- The domain of the business knowledge.
- The project experience of the subject matter experts (SMEs) and implementation team.

It is therefore impossible for me to provide a standard one-size-fits-all set of model coefficients here.

However, the key message is that DRA provides quantitative measures that can be plugged into a model to provide estimates of project effort. When the model is first used it will be based purely on professional judgments, and so the estimates will carry a relatively high level of uncertainty, although probably still less than would result from any alternative approach. This uncertainty must be reflected in your project contingency. As your organization acquires experience by executing a number of knowledge automation projects, the model can be tuned for your particular project methodology, architecture, business domain, and team, using statistics collected from completed projects.

If you are using an iterative or agile methodology it can also be fine-tuned *during* a project, by monitoring progress and comparing the expended effort with the expected burn rate.

DRA in Estimation

The following can all be used as predictors of effort:

- The number of *decision points*.
- The number of *decision nodes* in scope.
- The number and complexity of the *data nodes* required.

> **DRA in Estimation** *(Continued)*
> - The number, type, and complexity of the *knowledge nodes* in scope.
> - The number of *arrows* linking decision nodes in scope.
>
> The most important indicators are the decision points and knowledge nodes.
> The model can be tuned for your team using statistics from completed projects or (under iterative project management) during a project. ■

Planning

A knowledge automation project can be defined as one that encapsulates business knowledge in decision services. The differentiating feature of such projects is the task of knowledge discovery: All of the knowledge to be automated must be collected, agreed on, and codified in an executable form. This task can be a major component of the project, with effort comparable to and sometimes exceeding the design and development tasks.

Knowledge discovery can be one of the major sources of risk in automation projects, because it is open-ended and often far too large to be managed as a single task. This risk cascades to the design and implementation tasks that are dependent on it. The solution is to use DRA to agree on the scope of automation *before knowledge discovery commences.* This allows the production of complete and detailed plans at the outset of a project with specific discovery, development, and testing tasks for each knowledge node on the DRD. The effort required for these tasks may be estimated using the results of DRAW, as described earlier.

There are two basic models for software development projects: waterfall and iterative. DRA can help in either approach.

Waterfall Models

In the waterfall approach, an implementation project goes through a sequence of phases, for example:

1. Requirements
2. Design
3. Development
4. Testing
5. Deployment

The central idea of waterfall approaches is that all the requirements are gathered and agreed on before any design is carried out, and all the design is completed before any development takes place. This philosophy is based on the observation that errors in requirements are much cheaper to fix before design has taken place, and errors in design are much cheaper to fix before development has started. The waterfall approach therefore stresses the importance of complete documentation of the results of each phase before moving on to the next (otherwise known as Big Design Up Front).

Issues are found with waterfall in practice, however, mainly because people find it very difficult to go through the design and construction phases without wanting to change the requirements. Design and development may take many months, so it is quite likely that the requirements will genuinely change during that time. People also learn from the experience of design and implementation, especially if the technology is novel to them; they see the original requirements in a different light and see opportunities to meet them in different ways. So over the past 20 years the software industry has gradually moved away from the pure waterfall model toward modified approaches, including iterative models.

A pure waterfall approach presents particular problems for a project with any significant amount of knowledge discovery. Codified business knowledge is, in principle, a set of requirements: It defines how the system should behave, that is, what decisions it should make. But a project plan in which all design and development waits for the knowledge discovery to be complete will be much longer than necessary and will not make good use of resources, because the knowledge discovery team (business experts and decision analysts) is usually entirely separate from the implementation team (designers, developers, and testers). The two groups could be working in parallel.

You will have gathered by now that I am not a big fan of the waterfall model for knowledge automation projects. However, if you are committed to this approach DRA is a very valuable tool for several reasons:

- It precisely identifies the areas of knowledge to be discovered during the requirements phase. This allows the requirements phase to be planned, rather than open-ended, and provides more confidence that the requirements are actually complete at the end of the phase.
- It provides a structure for the design phase, allowing the design to be broken into functional components based on the DRDs, and providing confidence that the design is complete at the end of the phase.

- It identifies all the data requirements, reducing the risk that additional integration points will be identified during the development or testing phases, resulting in costly rework of the requirements and design.
- It provides a very clear definition of the scope of the automated decisions in the automation scoping document, against which testing can be coordinated.

DRA, therefore, mitigates the worst features of the waterfall model, and substantially reduces the risks of rework and overrun often associated with waterfall projects.

Iterative Models

Iterative models are an attempt to address the problems seen with waterfall by breaking the project into a series of mini-projects, or iterations. Each iteration addresses all the phases of the software lifecycle—requirements, design, construction, and testing—to implement an increment of functionality. There is a spectrum of iterative approaches, from phased to agile, differing chiefly in the lengths of the iterations and the nature of the increments. Over recent years, as the concepts have become more pervasive, the industry has experimented with shorter and shorter iterations.

The problems with the waterfall model are turned into virtues with an iterative approach: The end of each iteration presents an opportunity for reevaluating the requirements and the design, and the team's growing familiarity with the technology is exploited over successive iterations. However, the virtues of waterfall can be vices in an iterative approach: The lack of a complete set of requirements at the outset means that projects have no clear completion criteria, which can result in scope creep, overruns, or in the worst case, abandoned projects.

DRA solves these problems by providing a basis for planning an iterative project with clearly defined increments and completion criteria. The principle is that the structure of the plan should reflect the structure of the decision-making to be automated, as revealed in the DRD. Increments of functionality may be defined very simply, by partitioning the nodes on the DRD into sets. The objectives of this partitioning are that:

- Each increment can be delivered in one phase or iteration: that is, the effort needed for knowledge discovery, design, and implementation (estimated as discussed earlier) is roughly the same for each increment, and achievable in the time allocated to the iteration.

- Each increment provides some distinct functional benefit to the organization, that is, the decisions made in each partition are useful to some extent in themselves, even if the final top-level decision is in another partition.
- The increments are loosely coupled; that is, there are few arrows connecting nodes in different partitions. Usually, this will mean that each decision node should be in the same increment as the knowledge node(s) it requires.
- The increments relate in a simple, convenient way to decision points, for example, one increment covers all the decisions for a number of decision points, or (more usually) one decision point is implemented in a number of increments.

Figure 5.1 shows how the decisions for a single decision point might be partitioned between a number of increments. Our example DRD from Figure 4.1 has been partitioned into three increments:

Increment 1: Risk
- Knowledge discovery: *Application risk scorecard* and *Risk matrices*
- Decision implementation: *Application risk score* and *Risk grade*
- Data integration: *Applicant details* and *Bureau data*

Increment 2: Affordability
- Knowledge discovery: *Repayment calculations*, *Affordability calculations*, and *Affordability rules*
- Decision implementation: *Monthly repayment*, *Disposable income*, and *Affordability*
- Data integration: *Requested loan*, *Interest rate*, and *Income and expenses*

Increment 3: Routing
- Knowledge discovery: *Security calculations*, *Eligibility rules*, and *Routing rules*
- Decision implementation: *Security*, *Eligibility*, and *Application routing*
- Data integration: *Applicant details*, *Bureau data*, *Property valuation*, and *Requested loan*

Note that the partitioning reveals what external data sources will be required by each increment for testing and integration of the delivered decision modules; they are the data nodes linked with arrows into decisions within the increment. They also reveal dependencies between the increments (for example, the *Application routing* decision in Increment 3 depends on the *Affordability* decision in Increment 2). These data and decision dependencies imply project task

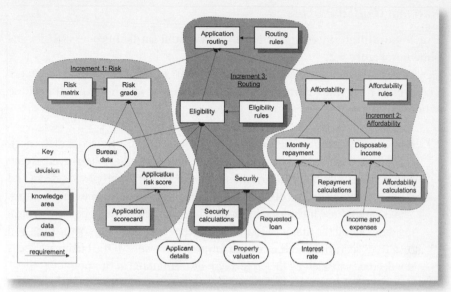

FIGURE 5.1   Partitioning the DRD into Increments

dependencies that must be represented in the plan. One of the intentions of the loose coupling objective in partitioning is to minimize the number of such dependencies.

The more agile your chosen methodology, the smaller the increments will be. I suggest that in most circumstances the smallest useful increment for a sprint would consist of a single decision node with all its knowledge areas, although it may sometimes be necessary to divide single knowledge areas up into multiple iterations if they are very large or complex (such as when rule sets are expected to contain hundreds of rules). When using increments based on single decisions I would advocate starting at the bottom of the DRD and working up, so that all the subdecisions required by the decision implemented in each sprint have already been implemented in previous sprints.

However, I favor larger-scale iterations with a duration of about three to six weeks. This gives time for administrative project tasks like knowledge review and sign-off and allows a natural rhythm to develop between the knowledge discovery and implementation teams. Remember that the business experts must also have some spare time to pursue their normal jobs; it is rare that they can be seconded full-time onto the knowledge automation project.

Rational Unified Process

One important iterative approach is the Rational Unified Process (RUP),[1] as shown in Figure 5.2.

Under RUP every project is divided into four phases. Each of these phases comprises one or more iterations and concludes with a well-defined milestone where critical project decisions are made:

1. *Inception.* The inception phase is concerned with defining the scope of the project and establishing the business case for it. Scope definition often involves use-case analysis: identifying all the interactions between the proposed system and other entities (users and other systems), and describing them with use cases. The business case includes a high-level plan of the following phases, including dates for all the major milestones, together with estimates of the time and resources required and the criteria for project success. If the business case is not deemed satisfactory the project can be terminated at this point.

   Milestone: Lifecycle Objectives

2. *Elaboration.* The principal purpose of the elaboration phase is to identify and eliminate the most significant project risks, especially technical ones. This

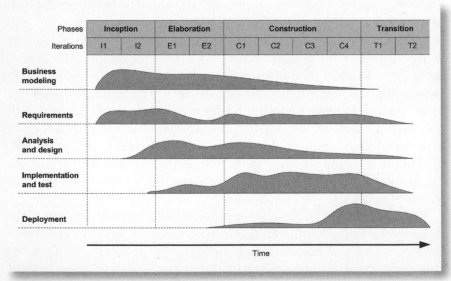

FIGURE 5.2 Rational Unified Process

Adapted from Rational Unified Process: Best Practices for Software Development Teams. Rational Software White Paper TP026B, Rev. 11/01.

involves analyzing the problem domain, establishing a sound architectural foundation, and creating a full and detailed project plan. A comprehensive system architecture is defined at a high level (the so-called mile wide and inch deep view of the system), along with its functional and nonfunctional requirements. The integration of the main components of the architecture is often demonstrated by building prototypes of limited functionality.

Milestone: Lifecycle Architecture

3. *Construction Phase:* In the construction phase, attention is turned from the development of intellectual property (requirements and specifications) to the development of deployable products. All the components of the architecture defined in the elaboration phase are now developed and integrated into the system and all features are tested thoroughly. Ideally, the construction phase is divided into a number of iterations such that each results in the delivery of a piece of functionality that has value in itself. By the end of the phase the entire system has been delivered.

Milestone: Initial Operational Capability

4. *Transition Phase:* The transition phase consists mainly of the activities required to pass the system into the hands of the user community. This includes not just software release but training and change management. However, it may also include further product development and deployment iterations if issues have been identified during construction or user testing or to cover features (usually changes to requirements) postponed from earlier phases.

Milestone: Product Release

Note that these phases are *not* equivalent to requirements, design, development, and test. Under RUP, requirements, design, development, and test are activities that occur in each phase and iteration.

In a project managed using RUP, DRAW is a natural part of the inception phase, since it helps to define the project scope. The results of DRAW, recorded in the automation scoping document, can then be used to help plan the following phases. Using DRA, a typical knowledge automation project plan under RUP would have the following high-level structure:

1. *Inception.* Agree on the project goals; establish the scope of automated decision-making using DRAW; establish the high-level technical and nonfunctional requirements; plan all subsequent phases and iterations using partitions drawn on the DRDs.

2. *Elaboration.* Establish the detailed technical requirements and demonstrate integration with the client architecture (e.g., BPMS) by building one or more empty prototype decision services, based on the integration requirements exposed by DRA.
3. *Construction.* Over a number of iterations, gradually add increments of functionality to the prototypes until all the decision services are complete, performing knowledge discovery and design as required for each increment.
4. *Transition.* Perform user testing, training and handover, placing responsibility for maintaining the business knowledge back in the hands of the domain experts.

Note the contrast between waterfall and RUP. Under waterfall, all the business knowledge is collected up front in the requirements phase before any design has occurred. Under RUP, knowledge discovery does not occur until the construction phase, after the high-level architectural design is complete and proven. It is carried out in each iteration, alongside the detailed design and implementation of the service components that encapsulate the knowledge.

DRA in Project Planning

DRA can be used under the waterfall approach, or an iterative project management technique such as RUP.
Under the waterfall approach:

- If DRAW has not been carried out before the project starts, make it the first task in the requirements phase.
- Use the automation scoping document as a definition of high-level requirements.
- Plan knowledge discovery tasks during the requirements phase for each knowledge area in the DRDs.
- Structure the design and implementation phases to deliver functional components based on the DRDs.
- Use the automation scoping document to control scope and to coordinate testing.

Under RUP:

- If DRAW has not been carried out before the project starts, make it the first task in the inception phase.

DRA in Project Planning *(Continued)*

- Use the automation scoping document as a definition of scope.
- Define a number of functional increments using partitions drawn on the DRDs. Plan knowledge discovery, design, development, and testing tasks for each increment.
- In the elaboration phase, prove integration with the client architecture by building one or more empty prototype decision services, based on the integration requirements exposed by DRA.
- In the construction phase, gradually add increments of functionality to the prototypes until all the decision services are complete. ■

 ## DRA IN KNOWLEDGE DISCOVERY

If you are familiar with the field of business rules, you might be surprised that I am well into the fifth chapter of this book and have only just started to discuss knowledge discovery. But that is as it should be: Knowledge discovery should not lead the process of knowledge automation but should fall out of it. This is especially true under RUP. The scope of your knowledge automation project has been agreed on using DRAW and depicted on a DRD; you have planned the project by partitioning the scope into a number of iterations with discrete discovery tasks for all the knowledge nodes in each; you have built empty prototype decision services to demonstrate the technical architecture is sound. *Now* you can start discovery, decision by decision, extending the functionality of the decision services as you go.

In any particular discovery task you are gathering only the knowledge required to make a particular decision at defined points in the business process. As I explained in Chapter 3, this decision-centric approach is considerably simpler than attempting to define abstract universal business knowledge that applies across all business processes and activities. For example, in Iteration 1 of Figure 5.1, you would be asking the domain experts to provide *only* the application risk scorecard and the matrix used to convert the risk score into a risk grade. This is a very well-defined work package, capable of being represented in a plan as two discrete tasks. *No other business knowledge should be solicited.*

The goal of each knowledge discovery task can be gleaned from the DRD and its node definitions, stating which decision nodes are supported by the knowledge node and what the inputs and outputs of those decisions are. Figure 5.3 shows the subgraph of the DRD relevant to the *Risk matrix* knowledge area. This knowledge node supports the *Risk grade* decision. During DRAW we defined

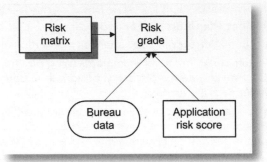

FIGURE 5.3 Knowledge Discovery Subgraph

this decision as taking *Bureau data* and the *Application risk score* subdecision as inputs, and providing a single risk category as a result (RG1, RG2, RG3, RG4, or RG5). The business knowledge to be collected must therefore be sufficient to provide a decision value of RG1, RG2, RG3, RG4, or RG5 under all circumstances, using only bureau data and application risk score. It must not refer to any other data or produce any other results.

The information in the partitioned DRD therefore specifies very precisely the set of knowledge discovery tasks to be carried out in each iteration of the project, and this structure can be used to configure whatever tool is used to collect the discovered knowledge. For example, even if using a generic spreadsheet product, one tab of the workbook can be allocated to each knowledge area and an index tab can list the discovery tasks, grouped by increment, with hyperlinks to the relevant worksheets. This index list can also be used for monitoring the progress of discovery over the course of the project. Table 5.1 shows

TABLE 5.1 Discovery Workbook Structure

Increment	Decision	Knowledge Area	Owner	Status
Risk	Application risk score	Application scorecard	Risk	Approved
	Risk grade	Risk matrix	Risk	Approved
Affordability	Monthly repayment	Repayment calculations	Risk	Approved
	Disposable income	Affordability calculations	Risk	Complete
	Affordability	Affordability rules	Risk	Ongoing
Routing	Security	Security calculations	Compliance	Not started
	Eligibility	Eligibility rules	Marketing	Not started
	Application routing	Routing rules	Marketing	Not started

what the index tab might look like during the affordability increment. The status column tracks the discovery process for each knowledge area and records when the discovered knowledge is approved by the subject matter experts for implementation.

If you are using a special-purpose knowledge discovery tool the configuration can be based more directly on the structure of the DRD, and templates can be provided for each type of knowledge supported by the BRMS.

DRA in Knowledge Discovery

Knowledge discovery should be broken into tasks corresponding to the knowledge nodes on the DRD.

In each discovery task you gather only the knowledge required to make a particular decision. No other business knowledge should be solicited.

The business knowledge collected must provide only the decision values defined for the decision, using only the data linked to the decision on the DRD. It must not refer to any other data or produce any other results.

Business knowledge can be collected in a workbook, with one tab per knowledge area. ■

The precise nature of each knowledge discovery task depends on the form of the knowledge to be collected. As discussed in Chapter 3, business knowledge may take the form of business rules, algorithms, or predictive analytic models.

Discovering Business Rules

There is a substantial body of literature on the art of business rule discovery, including the seminal works by Ronald Ross[2] and Barbara Von Halle,[3] and I don't want to add much to it except to observe that a lot of the problems evaporate if the process is properly guided and constrained using an iterative, decision-centric approach. Rule discovery should never be open-ended, it should be organized into discrete tasks, each with a specific goal: establishing the business rules for a particular decision.

This makes the process of discovery much simpler. The business domain experts can be asked a very specific question, for example (referring again to Figure 5.1), "What are the rules for deciding whether the application is eligible?" They have already discussed this decision at a high level in the DRAW sessions, where they agreed that this decision was necessary and what information it required, so the rules discovery task is one of probing for a more detailed definition of the knowledge area: a full set of business rules for the decision.

You are aiming to define a rule set that is complete and consistent, as discussed in Chapter 3. As you gather the rules you should also ensure that each rule is atomic, precise, concise, and independent (or declarative). Here is a brief explanation of these six key attributes of a well-tempered rule set:

1. *Completeness.* A set of rules is complete if it is sufficient to make a decision in all possible scenarios. Since you have already established the nature of the decision's results, you may be able to elicit rules by asking the experts questions like, "When would the decision take *this* value?" especially if the decision is categorical and you have a list of all its possible values. But it is not enough to collect rules that cover all possible *conclusions*; completeness requires that all possible *conditions* are covered (such that at least one rule fires, whatever set of data is presented to the rule set). So you will also be asking, "What decision would be made under *these* conditions?"

2. *Consistency.* A set of rules is consistent if the rules are mutually exclusive (only one rule fires in any particular scenario) or there is some clear system for resolving conflicts (such as priorities associated with decision values). To check for inconsistencies, look for rules that have the same or overlapping conditions but have different conclusions. For example, "IF height < 2.0 THEN size = short" is inconsistent with "IF height > 1.8 THEN size = tall" over the range 1.8 to 2.0, unless it is stated which of these sizes takes precedence when multiple rules fire.

3. *Atomicity.* A rule is atomic if it is stated in its simplest form. In particular, it is good practice to avoid disjunctions (the use of "or" between conditions). The disjunctive rule "IF a or b THEN x" should be restated as two separate atomic rules: "IF a THEN x" and "IF b THEN x." This makes the rules easier to understand, easier to maintain, and easier to test. An exception is usually made where the conditions are checking multiple values of the same property (for example, in "IF month = May, June, July, or August").

4. *Precision.* The conditions of each rule should be precise in stating exactly what the domain expert intends. For example, in the rule "IF age > 25 THEN status = mature" what do we mean by "> 25"? Is 25 years and 3 months enough, or must it be 26? And more subtly, at what date are we measuring age: the date of application, the current date, or the service commencement date? If this rule is evaluated at multiple decision points, on different dates, should it always produce the same result?

5. *Conciseness.* Rules should be concise (that is, use only the minimum number of conditions required to identify the set of cases covered by the rule). The logic in the rule "IF age > 18 and age > 16 THEN x" entails that the second condition is redundant, but in "IF relation = sister and gender = female" we recognize the second condition as redundant only because we are familiar with the meaning of "sister." Things may not always be so obvious when we are dealing with esoteric business terms. A similar concern applies across the rules in a rule set: if there are two rules "IF age > 16 THEN x" and "IF age > 18 THEN x," the second rule is redundant.

6. *Independence.* Rules should be stated in such a way that they are independent of each other and of the order of evaluation. It is not safe to have two rules "IF risk < 500 THEN grade = low" and "IF risk < 700 THEN grade = medium" and assume that the first rule will filter out the low cases before the medium rule is applied. The second rule should be "IF risk >= 500 and risk < 700 THEN grade = medium." It should be possible for the rules in the set to be evaluated in any order yet produce the same results.

Attributes of a Well-Tempered Rule Set

Rules should be:

1. *Complete:* sufficient to make a decision in all possible scenarios.
2. *Consistent:* either the rules are mutually exclusive or there is some clear system for conflict resolution.
3. *Atomic:* stated in their simplest form.
4. *Precise:* stating exactly what the domain expert intends.
5. *Concise:* using only the minimum number of conditions required to identify the set of cases covered by the rule.
6. *Independent:* stated in such a way that they do not depend on each other or the order of evaluation. ▪

These attributes are considerably simpler to achieve if a metaphor is used for the rule set, such as a decision table or decision tree, as described in Chapter 3. In a decision table, all the rules have conditions based on the same terms, so completeness and consistency can be checked by filtering on the values in the columns. A decision tree is usually created by gradually adding nodes that test one or more conditions; as long as all possible values are covered by the paths out of every node (for example, by using an "otherwise" condition), the tree is guaranteed to be complete.

In accordance with the decision-centric approach, you should also be checking the scope as you collect the rules:

- The rules should only determine results relevant to the decision in focus.
- The rules should only use terms in the data areas available to the decision in the DRD.

If the subject matter experts propose rules that determine new decision values or use new areas of data, an extension to scope may need to be agreed on.

Of course, the conditions of business rules do not refer to *areas* of data, as shown in the DRD, but business terms corresponding to specific *items* of data in those areas. As detail is provided to the knowledge nodes in the form of specific rules, the data nodes related to them will also be provided with detail in the form of specific business terms. These terms will be picked up in the design activity (remember, this is a parallel activity, not a later stage) and used to extend the object model, usually by adding properties to objects.

If data areas are used by multiple decisions they must be cross-checked to ensure that reused terms genuinely refer to the same item, and that multiple terms are not being used for the same item in different rule sets. When all the knowledge areas are fully specified, the full set of business terms, collected and rationalized, comprises a complete specification of the input data required by the decision services.

As well as providing a complete set of rules, the experts should be asked to provide test cases for them. Not the exhaustive set of unit test cases the developers will be creating as part of implementation but a few characteristic cases representing typical business scenarios where they can state with confidence the correct decision values to be returned. Ideally, these should be real cases taken from historical data. These characteristic cases should cover a range of decision values. For example, if the decision is categorical, there should be at least one test case in each category. These characteristic cases have multiple uses: They help to clarify questions arising during analysis, they will be used by the implementation team as templates for more detailed tests, and they will eventually be employed directly in user testing.

A note of caution: Remember that the goal is not necessarily to discover and automate all the business rules *currently used* in the organization, but to define a set that will implement a set of *optimal* corporate policies considered and agreed on by the domain experts. In 2005, I started working with a large health insurer in Ireland on a system to support and automate health care claims assessment. On my first day in Dublin I asked an adjudicator to take me through the process of assessing a claim. She picked up the top claim form from the substantial pile on her desk and started to say, "Well, first we check this section . . ." Then she stopped, and said, "Well, of course, we would just pay this one." "Why?" I enquired, eager to collect my first business rule. She stared at me with disbelief. "Well, she's a *nun*, isn't she?"

I'm glad to report this particular rule did not find its way into the final *Assess claim* decision service.

Discovering Algorithms

Since algorithms are used principally where the business knowledge is inherently procedural, it makes sense to capture algorithms as procedures using pseudocode. Following our decision-centric approach, you will be asking the business experts to define procedures that will calculate the decision results and will work downward from there using subprocedures as necessary. Keeping an eye on scope, as always, all terms used in the procedures must either be items from data areas included in the DRD partition for this increment or must be derived by a subprocedure from such data.

Algorithms must be complete in exactly the same way as rule sets: They must provide a decision result under all possible combinations of values of their input data. When algorithms contain branch points based on logical conditions, other desirable attributes of rules apply to some extent. For example, such conditions should be stated atomically, precisely, and concisely. But there are other attributes specific to algorithms, for example, that boundary conditions on loops are correctly stated.

But most of the guidelines for this activity are simply those of good program design (relaxed somewhat for the purposes of knowledge discovery). For example, you should generalize procedures and reuse them across multiple algorithms wherever possible. I don't think it is necessary to elaborate on these here.

Discovering Analytic Models

Analytic models are not discovered from human experts but from empirical data. The business knowledge in such models is used to make automated decisions but is itself the output of another decision management process: predictive analytic modeling. This modeling process takes large quantities of historical case data and produces knowledge, in the form of models, as output. These basic principles of predictive analytics were explained in Chapter 3.

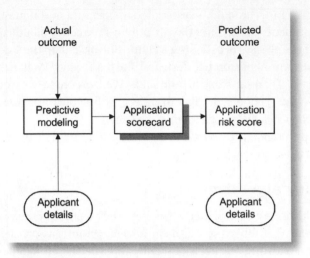

FIGURE 5.4 Discovering the Analytic Model

Figure 5.4 shows the relationship between analytics and automation for the *Application scorecard* knowledge node in Figure 5.1. The predictive modeling process looks at a large number of historical cases, comparing applicant details with the eventual outcome of each case to discover the features that best predict the outcome from the applicant details. These features are expressed as an application scorecard. This scorecard can then be used by the *Application risk score* decision to predict the likely outcome for each case, based on the current applicant details. Creating a predictive analytic model can take weeks or months, depending on the complexity of the data and the number of data items available. However, with careful planning, modeling and implementation can take place in parallel, as long as DRA has identified the requirements for such a model in advance.

Note that for the model to be an effective predictor, the data used in the decision on each case must be the *same set of items* as those used to create the model. Before modeling, you will not know which items will be most predictive. However, if your data collection process is fixed, you know from the analysis of the decision points what data will be available at the point where the model is first used by a decision. This is the set of data from which you can select characteristics to build the model. On the other hand, if the process is flexible, you can use a wider set of data for modeling, find the most predictive characteristics, and change the process so that all the data are available at the time the decision needs to be made. Sometimes a process of negotiation takes place, with the marketing department wanting to include extra fields in the application form to improve customer scoring, and operations wanting to remove them to streamline the new automated process.

A final point of detail: Predictive models are never built on the entire population of cases; certain types of cases are excluded because they are untypical and would distort the results (for example, fraudulent cases and bankruptcies). All these exclusions must be dealt with appropriately in the decision service. One common solution is to carry out scoring on all cases but implement the exclusions later as eligibility rules; another is to include the exclusion rules in the scorecard, recorded in special symbolic values of the score. With either approach, cases excluded from scoring are generally declined.

 ## DRA IN DESIGN

Design tends to be the prerogative of technical architects and reflects their concerns and values. It tends to be elegant from the bottom up: that is, it implements the required functionality using the computational resources very efficiently. However, such designs can sometimes be difficult for the non–technically minded to fathom, and it is vitally important when encapsulating business knowledge that the business users are able to understand how their knowledge is represented and how it is applied in the decision service. After all, they are going to be expected to maintain the knowledge over time. So for decision services, good design should also be elegant from the top down: the structure of the solution should be parsimonious and reflect the structure of the decision-making.

Bottom-up design is very specific to the platform, anyway, so it is not easy to discuss such issues in this book, which is intended to be product-neutral. Top-down design, however, can be purely functional. So although performance is important, I will be focusing in this section on the structural aspects of the design. My proposal is that the structure of decision-making revealed in the DRD should be used as the basis for designing a set of decision services, their decision flows, and the object model they use.

Allocating Decision Services to Decision Points

The default assumption is that there will be one decision service implementing each decision point in the business process, but this is not always the case, because decision services may be reused over multiple decision points. Indeed, as we observed in Chapter 2, this reuse of decision logic is one of the goals of automation. It is also possible for a single decision point to be implemented with multiple decision services, each providing a component of the required decision-making. The allocation of decision services to decision points is a design judgment, not a functional requirement. Here are some guidelines on how to make that judgment.

For each decision point in the business process flow, identify in the DRD all the principal decisions that were defined in the DRAW, all their subdecisions, and all the knowledge and data nodes supporting those decisions. This subgraph defines the total extent of the decision-making to be implemented in the decision services to be called at that decision point. Compare the various decision point subgraphs, looking for areas of overlap (nodes that appear in multiple decision points).

If there are no overlaps, as in Figure 5.5, the design judgment is simple: each subgraph can be implemented as a separate decision service, mapping one-to-one with the corresponding decision point.

If there are small areas of overlap, as in Figure 5.6 (for example, one or two decisions that appear in two decision points), the decision points should probably still be implemented as separate decision services. You have two design options: the results of these shared decisions can be persisted by the BPMS after the first decision point and provided to the second decision point as data, or the decisions can be evaluated independently at both decision points. The approach you choose will depend on a number of factors, including whether the data might change between the decision points.

Even if decisions are evaluated in multiple services, the knowledge areas used for those decisions should be reused. The BRMS maintains a repository of all the

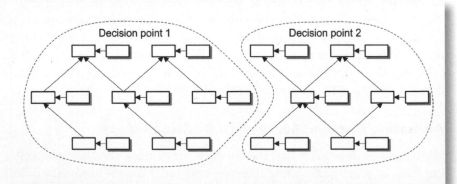

FIGURE 5.5 Decision Point Subgraphs with No Overlap

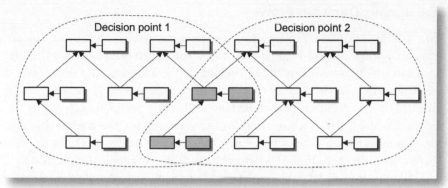

FIGURE 5.6 Decision Point Subgraphs with Small Overlap

business knowledge in the DRD, and deploys a subset of it in each decision service (see Figure 3.3). Knowledge areas can therefore be reused simply by deploying them in multiple services. Basing the structure of the repository and the design of the decision services on the decision structure revealed by DRA makes this reuse of business knowledge easy and natural.

If there is a large or total overlap between two decision point subgraphs, as in Figure 5.7, they should be implemented with a single decision service. Any slight differences between the two subgraphs can be accommodated by logic in the service that chooses which decisions to evaluate. The decision service therefore needs to be told which decision point it is being called from; this decision point identifier should always be provided in the data passed to a decision service.

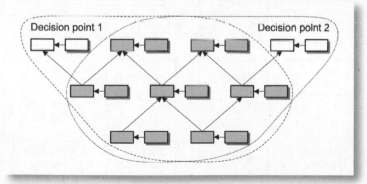

FIGURE 5.7 Decision Point Subgraphs with Large Overlap

Designing Decision Flows

Many BRMS and other implementation environments, especially those that are predominantly forward-chaining, provide some mechanism for specifying the order in which decisions should be evaluated. If you are working with such an environment you need to convert the network of dependencies represented in the DRD into a procedure or decision flow. In this brief section I suggest a simple method for doing this. If you are working in a predominantly backward-chaining environment this may be unnecessary; the arrows representing dependencies between the decisions in the DRD may be used directly as rules for chaining.

Having prepared the subgraph for each decision service, strip it of all nodes except the decisions. The arrows between these nodes specify a *partial ordering* of the decisions to be evaluated by this service. This reduced network can be simplified further by removing tautological dependencies: whenever two decisions are connected both directly and indirectly, remove the direct connection. The partial ordering shown in Figure 5.8 has been derived in this way from the example DRD used in Figure 5.1.

In some BRMS this partial ordering may be sufficient for the decision flow, but others will require you to reduce it to a linear flow with no parallel tasks. You can linearize the partial ordering simply by choosing an arbitrary sequence for any parallel nodes. (There could be many possible sequences that are compatible with the partial ordering.) The result, as shown in Figure 5.9, is a decision flow for a service to implement the decision point subgraph. Each

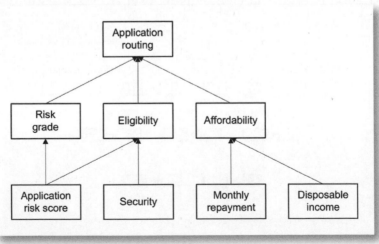

FIGURE 5.8   Partial Ordering of Decisions

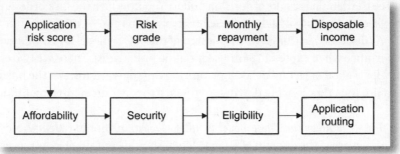

FIGURE 5.9 One Possible Decision Flow

task in this flow must trigger the evaluation of the decision by the BRMS by applying the appropriate business knowledge.

There are three situations in which you might need to extend this simple approach:

1. This method assumes that all the data are provided to the service in the call so are not relevant to the decision flow. This will usually be the case for a typical stateless decision service. If, in spite of my advice in Chapter 2, you require the service to call out to other systems to acquire data (e.g., by querying a database), the data nodes should also be included in the ordering analysis.

2. If you are reusing a decision service for decision points that do not have total overlap of functionality (as in Figure 5.7), there will be decisions that are not in scope at certain decision points. You will then need to elaborate the linear sequence in Figure 5.9 with branches for conditional subflows to ensure that only the relevant decisions are evaluated at each decision point.

3. Finally, if any decisions are made for multiple instances of objects (e.g., selecting and configuring a list of possible offers), your decision flow may contain loops to evaluate the necessary decisions for each instance in the list.

But provided the decisions are evaluated in a sequence that is compatible with the partial ordering implied by the DRD, it is guaranteed that every decision will have all the information it needs (input data and the results of subdecisions) when it is evaluated by the decision service.

Designing Object Models

During knowledge discovery, you should have identified all the business terms referred to by the rules, algorithms, and models, and associated them with nodes in the DRD. Input terms will be associated with data nodes; output terms will be the detailed results of decision nodes. You now face the task of designing an object model into which all these business terms can be mapped.

As discussed in Chapter 3, the design of the object model is of fundamental importance when expressing knowledge as business rules. There are two objectives for a good object model design, one looking upward toward the business domain, the other looking downward toward the technical implementation:

1. *The structure of the object model should be logical:* It should reflect the logical structure of the domain of knowledge. It should contain objects representing things naturally discussed in the business domain and describe the relationships between those things. When the object model accurately reflects the domain, rules are much more easily expressed by the domain experts, more intelligible to analysts, easier to implement, more efficient to execute, and simpler to maintain. When considered as a "fact model" the importance of the object model is clear: Any knowledge not represented in the object model must be included explicitly in the rules.

2. *The structure of the object model should be event-based:* It should reflect the process steps that generate and consume data. Data become available in packets at particular points in the business process (for example, when a screen is submitted or when a database is queried), and are used in packets (for example, when passed to a decision service or displayed on a screen). These packets are the natural unit of reuse for data within the business process. In addition, the response time of a typical decision service call is largely determined by the efficiency of the data interface, so the object model for a service should only describe those items that are available and those that are used.

Both of these design objectives must be considered, but there is often some tension between them, sometimes to the extent that it can be difficult to satisfy both in the same model. This problem is felt especially when there are a number of distinct objects, and different properties of a single object (for example, the applicant) arise at a number of different points in the process flow. When conflicts arise, how should you weigh up the best option? Is a compromise possible?

I have no hesitation in saying that on the input side of the object model (the data being passed into the decision service) the logical structure is much more important than the event structure. There is a range of purely technical solutions to the reuse and efficiency issues, which depend on the solution architecture and are well beyond the scope of this book. But the *trueness* of the object model to the domain is central to the purpose of the decision service in encapsulating business knowledge and cannot be compromised.

The principle of top-down with look-ahead can be useful here. When leading DRAW, the savvy decision analyst will be thinking about the likely structure of the object model and will try to define data areas for the DRD that demarcate groups of data that both relate to a single object and arise from the same event. The designer will then find it easier to arrange these in a logical and efficient object model.

On the output side (that is, the results being passed back by the service) the issue is not so clear-cut. Although the results concern objects in the domain, the fact they are the results of particular decisions taken at particular decision points is of vital relevance when they are used, especially if they are used by subsequent decision points. A single logical property of an object (such as a risk assessment of an individual) might be returned from multiple decision points; a subsequent decision point needs to distinguish between these and might even need to compare the different values against each other. For this reason I usually favor structuring the output side of the object model primarily by decision point and then by object and decision.

Figure 5.10 shows the skeleton of an object model for the simple DRD in Figure 4.1, defined as an XML Schema Definition (XSD). Any real object model would be considerably more complex than this, but this diagram shows the basic structure. There are two principal objects: Data and Decisions. All the data areas in the DRD are represented as properties of the Data object, and all the decisions in the DRD are represented as properties of the Decisions object. Each of the properties of Data is itself an object with a number of properties, one for each data item in the data area; for example, the ApplicantDetails object would include a property for each piece of data describing the applicant. Similarly, each of the properties of the Decisions object is an object with a number of properties, one for each item of data in the decision results.

The model shown in Figure 5.10 defines a top-level Request object. When the decision service is called it would be passed a message containing an instance of this object—a Request—with all the data properties populated with case data. As it made its decisions, the decision service would populate the decision properties and when complete it would pass back a message containing the whole structure: data and decisions. For this reason the data properties are compulsory and the decision properties are optional in the model. (This is only one possible way to use messaging with a decision service, an alternative is to have two separate messages, one for the request and another for the response.)

When making decisions that depend on the results of other decisions, the service will refer to values previously populated in the Decisions object. This makes the dependencies clear in the business logic. When decision values are

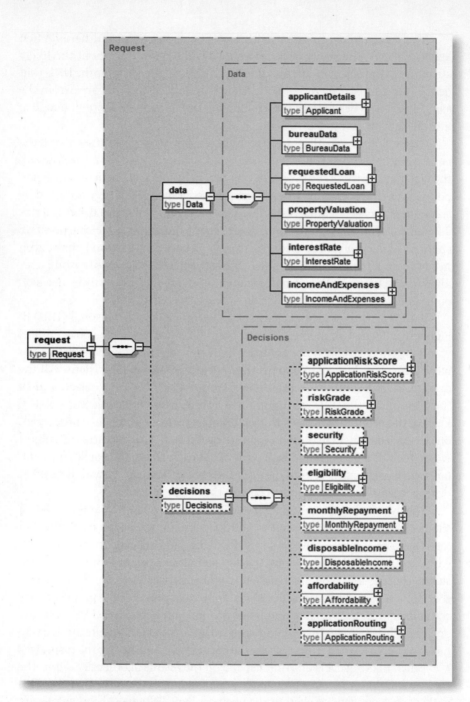

FIGURE 5.10 An Object Model

persisted externally and passed back into subsequent decision points, they should be presented back to those subsequent decision points in exactly the same structure (that is, in Decision objects not Data objects). A safe (but sometimes costly) approach is that all the decision results from each decision point are presented to every subsequent decision point.

Apart from the design of the structure of the object model, there is the issue of *which* data should be represented in it. On the input side, there are two extreme positions:

1. Include only the data used in the decision-making. This minimizes the size of the object model and thereby reduces the size of the messages passed to the decision service, which is one of the most important determiners of performance.
2. Include all data available at the time the decision service is called. This maximizes the agility of the solution, because new rules may be added at any time using a knowledge maintenance interface without the software changes required to extend the data interface.

Usually, the solution adopted will be some form of compromise between these two, including in the object model those data items that are *likely* at some time to be useful in rules. Certainly, you should never include in the model items that will never be used in decision-making. I once had quite a difficult discussion with a client who wanted to include all the data describing the applicant, including the individual's ethnic background. He eventually relented, but only when I pointed out that it would actually be illegal to use this item for any purpose in decision-making, so it should not be made available to the users for inclusion in business rules.

On the output side, there are again two extremes:

1. Include only the results of the principal decisions identified in the DRAW. This minimizes the size of the object model while providing the decisions required of the service by the business process.
2. Include all results determined by the decision service, including the results of all subdecisions and any intermediate values used in their derivation. This allows auditing of the entire decision-making process and is especially useful for debugging during testing.

Again, a compromise is usually called for. I normally advocate returning the results of all decisions in the DRD but not necessarily their internal, intermediate calculations unless these have significance to the business users.

> ### DRA in Design
>
> B ase the structure of the design on the structure of the decision-making as revealed in the DRD.
>
> Allocate decision services to decision points by determining the areas of overlap between the DRD subgraphs for each decision point.
>
> In backward-chaining BRMS, use the dependencies in the DRD as chaining rules; in forward-chaining BRMS, use them to find the partial ordering of decisions, and linearize it to produce a decision flow.
>
> If possible, design an object model that reflects both the structure of the domain knowledge and the events that generate and consume data. ■

 ## DRA IN IMPLEMENTATION

As shown in Figure 3.3, at the heart of the BRMS is a repository to store business knowledge from which decision services are deployed. A range of tools and facilities surround the repository, typically including:

- Facilities to configure the structure of the repository
- Facilities to edit business logic directly in the repository
- Facilities to create business user interfaces that allow subject matter experts to define and maintain their knowledge in the repository
- Facilities to import and edit predictive analytic models
- A business rules engine to execute business knowledge
- Tools to develop decision services encapsulating the knowledge in the repository
- Tools to test and deploy the decision services

The role of the SME is to provide and maintain the business knowledge. The role of the architect and development team is to set up all of the supporting infrastructure: creating and configuring the repository, providing facilities for the SMEs to enter their knowledge, and developing means of deploying the decision services.

Infrastructure Development

The first task is to install the BRMS product and set up the development, test, and production environments. The architect can then create the repository, set up deployment mechanisms, and development can start on any special interfaces required. As soon as the architect has defined the mapping between decision points and decision services, a full set of empty decision services can be created for integration testing. If web services are used it is not necessary to have the full object model defined at this stage (because WSDL [Web Services Description Language] specifies the data interface simply as a string); a high-level structure with a couple of input data fields and a single decision is usually perfectly adequate for this purpose. If the project is being run under RUP, this should all be done in the elaboration phase.

The team can then create a decision flow for each service, following the design, and define an "implementation type" for each decision task in the flows. The implementation type will be either a standard type (such as a simple rule set, metaphor, or function), or a bespoke type to be created specifically for this project. The implementation type defines:

- A format for the knowledge
- Templates for the knowledge maintenance interface
- A standard approach to implementation, with reusable code
- Reusable objects for inclusion in the object model
- A standard approach to testing

It will be a great advantage in implementation if the functionality required by decision tasks in the decision flow is largely satisfied by the capabilities of the standard implementation types. This is partly the responsibility of the decision analyst: as proposed in Chapter 4, the analyst should decompose the requirement using top-down with look-ahead. Some BRMS products are able to execute only certain types of knowledge (for example, some are based mainly on decision tables, others mainly on rules). The standard implementation types should therefore be aligned with the capabilities of the BRMS to be used for implementation, and the decision analyst should know what these are when conducting DRAW.

This repertoire will gradually grow. The development team will start with a few standard implementation types that have standard means of implementation in the BRMS (for example, an algorithm type implemented as a function call, a business rules type implemented as the application of a single rule set, and a number of supported metaphors). As the team implements successive projects it should develop a library of custom implementation types. Those that are seen to have repeated use can be generalized and added to the repertoire of standard types. Over time, an organization will develop a toolbox of standard execution patterns tailored to its particular decision-making style, which will allow reuse of design and code. This will also allow the SMEs to become familiar with the standard knowledge formats and understand when each should be used.

Some common decision patterns, suitable for inclusion in a repertoire of standard implementation types, are provided in Chapter 6.

Knowledge Configuration

As discussed in Chapter 1, one important dimension of decision yield (the benefit of implementing decision management) is increased agility in changing operational strategy. When the strategy has been automated as business rules in a BRMS, agility depends on how rapidly those rules can be updated and redeployed. However slick the knowledge editing facilities of the BRMS, operational agility is seriously compromised if changes to the rules are implemented using a conventional IT development cycle of change request, specification, implementation, and test. It is therefore important to separate maintenance into two tiers, so that certain constrained knowledge maintenance activities can be carried out safely by the business rather than by IT.

BRMS usually provide a facility for creating special knowledge maintenance interfaces for use by SMEs. Such interfaces are tailored to the form and scope of the knowledge in a particular knowledge area and allow the SME to edit *only the knowledge*, not the infrastructure that executes it, which remains the preserve of the IT development team. This exploits the nature of executable knowledge: the knowledge is reduced to the status of data for the system that executes it. It can therefore be updated using controls similar to those used to protect data in a database (levels of authority, password protection, etc.), rather than those used to control the release of software.

The interface facilities should be grouped for access according to the business functions responsible for maintaining the knowledge areas, as in Figure 5.11. This is based on the example DRD in Figure 4.1, but with the knowledge areas grouped for maintenance according to the responsibilities defined in the Owner column of Table 5.1. The infrastructure for the decisions that execute these knowledge areas remains the responsibility of the development team.

Knowledge maintenance interfaces are easier to use than a full development environment, because knowledge is edited using templates that are deliberately constrained so that the user is simply not able to commit syntactic errors. DRA allows these templates to be designed very specifically, by identi-

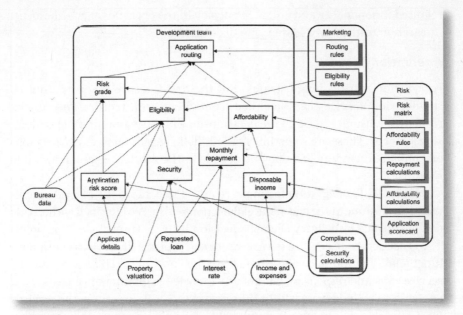

FIGURE 5.11 Knowledge Maintenance Interfaces

fying a set of discrete knowledge areas to be maintained by SMEs. DRA also identifies which data are required by the decisions using the knowledge, and when those data are available. If the knowledge maintenance templates are constrained so that the data items provided for inclusion in the rules are only those that are available when the decision will be evaluated, run-time errors caused by missing data will also be precluded.

The initial configuration of the business knowledge may be created by the development team or the SMEs, but in either case should use the knowledge maintenance interface rather than the full development environment. This provides a useful check that the templates are adequate and convenient. A good approach is that the knowledge is configured by the SMEs while supported by the development team; this allows the SMEs to become familiar with the use of the knowledge maintenance interfaces before they are handed over by the development team to the business.

Testing

As with any software implementation project, there are three levels of testing that must be carried out to demonstrate that the decision services provide the required functionality and are safe to deploy in the operational environment: integration testing, unit testing, and user testing.

Integration Testing

Integration testing demonstrates that the architecture is sound, that is, the decision services can be called from client architecture and results returned, without regard to the decision-making functionality of the decision services. These are sometimes called "hello world" tests, due to developers' habit of including just one line of code in the service to return a simple response.

Under RUP, integration testing is required to achieve the lifecycle architecture milestone at the end of the elaboration phase. As described earlier, this can be satisfied by delivery of empty decision services for each decision point. The exact degree of emptiness varies between projects. If services contain no functionality at all they can demonstrate the run-time architecture (that is, service calls and responses), but not any knowledge maintenance facilities. If you wish to include these within the scope of integration testing, the services need some decision-making content, however simple, configurable through a knowledge maintenance interface.

In the simplest case, this can consist of a single rule using a single input data item and returning a single decision value (e.g., IF age < 18 THEN routing = DECLINE). The knowledge maintenance interface needs only to allow the age limit in the rule to be varied. The architecture can then be demonstrated by using the knowledge maintenance interface to change the age limit, calling the decision service with cases of different ages, and observing that they are accepted or declined appropriately for the currently configured age limit.

Unit Testing

Unit testing demonstrates that each component in the decision services behaves correctly in isolation—that is, it makes the correct decisions—without regard to integration of this decision-making with the rest of the architecture.

The correctness of decisions is checked by reference to the knowledge defined in the knowledge discovery tool. There are special considerations for business rules, where we must demonstrate that each and every individual rule is correctly implemented but do not wish to test for every possible combination of values of the input data, which would, in most cases, be impractical. Instead we want to define a minimal set of tests for each rule, designed to exercise all of its principle modes of behavior. As a general principle, these tests will include:

- For conjunctions (conditions connected by "and"):
  - One positive test case, which fires the rule when all the conditions of the rule are satisfied
  - One negative test case for each condition of the rule, which fails to satisfy the condition and thus fails to fire the rule
- For disjunctions (conditions connected by "or"):
  - One negative test case, which fails to satisfy any of the conditions and thus fails to fire the rule
  - One positive test case for each condition of the rule, which satisfies the condition and thus fires the rule

As stated earlier, it is not best practice to include disjunctions in rules, but this may occur when a condition tests a single value against a list of possibilities (for example, employment status = STUDENT or UNEMPLOYED or SELF-EMPLOYED).

Note this approach results in $(n + 1)$ tests for a conjunctive rule with n Boolean conditions as opposed to n^2. So, for example, if a rule's conditions were "IF a and b and c THEN . . ." the test cases would include:

- a TRUE, b TRUE, c TRUE: rule fires.
- a FALSE, b TRUE, c TRUE: rule does not fire.
- a TRUE, b FALSE, c TRUE: rule does not fire.
- a TRUE, b TRUE, c FALSE: rule does not fire.

Similarly, if a rule's conditions were "IF a or b or c THEN . . ." the test cases would include:

- a FALSE, b FALSE, c FALSE: rule does not fire.
- a TRUE, b FALSE, c FALSE: rule fires.
- a FALSE, b TRUE, c FALSE: rule fires.
- a FALSE, b FALSE, c TRUE: rule fires.

A convenient approach is to use a standard generic case as a benchmark. Each test case will then specify:

- One or more small changes to the benchmark case data intended to create the desired combination of conditions

- The expected result: the value of the decision produced by the action function of the rule

Unit testing involves large numbers of such tests, and therefore requires the use of an automated testing facility that runs through all the defined tests calling the decision-making component and checks the actual results against the expected results. BRMS products usually provide such a tool.

User Testing

User testing demonstrates that the entire system behaves correctly as seen by the end users, with regard to integration and decision-making but without necessarily exhaustively covering all possible cases. It may include end-to-end testing, calling all the decision services in sequence from the BPMS using complete data sets.

User testing is typically based on a much smaller number of tests than unit testing but demands that these be characteristic of real cases and designed to cover all possible flows through the business process flow. The test cases should therefore be chosen to cover the possible results of the principal decisions defined in Stage 2 of DRAW (see Chapter 4). So the cases for the example in Figure 4.5 might include:

- Cases that would be declined with prebureau data
- Cases that require bureau data
- Cases that require no bureau data
- Cases that would be declined with bureau data
- Cases that would be referred for review
- Cases that are eligible in principle but receive no offers
- Cases that are eligible in principle and receive offers

Each test case will consist of the input data and the expected results and must be defined by the business to ensure that they are plausible for real cases. Note that since they are based on the results of DRAW the business can start to prepare these test cases early in the project. The cases can then be used as a resource during discovery, design, and implementation and used as the basis for the tests used by the development team for unit testing. This approach of starting with the test cases, rather than leaving them until the end of the project, is a hallmark of the agile approach to software development.

DRA in Implementation

Base the implementation of decisions mainly on a repertoire of standard implementation types, each defining:

- A format for the knowledge
- Templates for the knowledge maintenance interface
- A standard approach to implementation with reusable code
- Reusable objects for inclusion in the object model
- A standard approach to testing

The standard implementation types will be supplemented by bespoke types created specifically for the project. Over time, bespoke types that are reused can be generalized and added to the repertoire of standard types.

Provide specific knowledge maintenance interfaces tailored to each knowledge area, allowing SMEs to edit only the knowledge not the execution infrastructure.

Group the knowledge maintenance interfaces according to the owner of the knowledge.

Base unit testing on a large number of synthetic cases, designed to check every condition of every rule.

Base user testing on a smaller number of real cases, selected to cover the possible results of the principal decisions defined in DRAW. ■

 ## THE KNOWLEDGE PRODUCTION LINE

Knowledge-based systems are traditionally seen as complex hand-crafted engines, requiring skilled and experienced knowledge engineers. But the right approach can reduce the amount of skill required by conceiving of the decision service as many similar components (rules) fitting into a bespoke framework. Experienced engineers may be required to build the framework, but mass production techniques can be used to manufacture the components. This is, of course, the insight that allowed Henry Ford to slash the costs of production of motor cars at the beginning of the twentieth century, and it can have similar benefits in decision automation today.

In a knowledge automation project you are actually creating two things:

1. A machine for making decisions
2. A production line for building the machine

The combination of DRA and RUP (or any other iterative approach to delivery) makes it possible to create a highly efficient production line for discovery, design, and implementation. In each iteration of the construction phase, a defined increment of business knowledge is collected, analyzed, codified, and encapsulated within decision services. This involves passing it through a number of stages, as shown in Table 5.2.

All of these stages have been discussed in this chapter. Completing all this work within a single iteration of a few weeks' duration can be a very tough call unless all the following can be guaranteed:

- A good analysis of the requirements, using DRAW, resulting in cleanly defined increments for implementation
- Regular iterations, allowing a work rhythm to develop
- Very good working relationships between all concerned: the SMEs, the analyst, the architect, and the development team
- Commitment from all to quality and timescales

However, when all of these are in place, the results are remarkable, and the project can be a joy to work on. Achieving these conditions for success is of course the responsibility of the project sponsors and project managers.

Another important benefit of a production line is traceability. Basing the unit of production on increments defined using DRA as sets of decisions and knowledge areas on the DRD, allows full traceability through the knowledge

TABLE 5.2 Stages in the Knowledge Production Line

Stage	Task	Description	Workers
1	Knowledge discovery	Discover and analyze business knowledge	Decision analyst and SMEs
2	Design	Design any new components of infrastructure (services, flows, tasks, knowledge maintenance interfaces)	Architect
3	Development	Implement infrastructure for new components, including knowledge maintenance interfaces	Developers
4	Knowledge configuration	Configure business knowledge	Developers and/or SMEs
5	Unit test	Test behavior of delivered components	All

production line, from the delivered components, back through the design and knowledge discovery records, right up to the original requirements in the automation scoping document. For example:

- Every delivered decision service implements a number of principal decisions in the DRD, made at one or more decision points in the business process flow.
- Every delivered decision flow implements a subgraph of the DRD.
- Every delivered decision-making task in the decision flows implements a decision node in the DRD.
- Every delivered knowledge component (e.g., rule set or analytic model) implements a single knowledge area in the knowledge discovery tool, which provides the detailed requirements for a knowledge node in the DRD.

This degree of traceability is rare in software development in general and especially rare in rule-based systems. As I said at the beginning of this chapter, it results from the use of *structure*—the structure of decision-making revealed in the DRD—to organize and define all the tasks in the knowledge production line.

 NOTES

1. Rational, "Rational Unified Process: Best Practices for Software Development Teams," Rational Software White Paper TP026B, rev. 11/01, 2001.
2. R. G. Ross, *Principles of Business Rule Approach* (Boston: Addison-Wesley Professional, 2003).
3. B. Von Halle, *Business Rules Applied: Building Better Systems Using the Business Rule Approach* (Hoboken, NJ: John Wiley & Sons, 2001).

CHAPTER SIX

Common Decision Patterns

I
N OUR TOP-DOWN JOURNEY FROM high-level business requirements to decision service implementation, we have now reached the basement. Like most basements, it contains a slightly random collection of items. My aim is to present some concrete examples of how decision-making is automated in a few specific situations, to provide some solid ground for the rather abstract principles discussed in the previous chapters, and to provide some tricks of the trade for those new to BRMS. First, I present some examples of common types of automated decision, then I close with a discussion of various ways to handle collaborative decision-making where humans and decision services need to cooperate to reach a decision.

 ## IMPLEMENTATION TYPES

They say there's no substitute for experience, and after you have conducted a few knowledge automation projects you see the same decision patterns cropping up again and again with minor variations. Recognizing these patterns saves a considerable amount of time in the analysis process and allows the use of a toolkit of standard implementation types for development, as discussed in Chapter 5. The simplest patterns are what we could call "primitives," consisting of just a single knowledge area in a standard format. These primitives include rule sets and metaphors, algorithms, and analytic models, as discussed in Chapter 3. Obviously all of these should be available as standard implementation types. But your toolkit should go further than this and reflect the individual decision-making style of the organization.

This section provides a few nonprimitive patterns that I come across frequently, which might also be useful components in a generalized toolkit of standard implementation types. This is not intended to be a complete list, just a small selection of useful examples.

Category with Reasons

Usage

A rule-based categorical decision is, in principle, a very simple thing: the selection of one of a discrete set of alternative categories. Such decisions are found in many contexts, and they are frequently used for routing decisions, where the result (typically accept, refer, or decline) is used by the BPMS to determine the sequence flow for the case. The template originations process shown in Figure 2.7 has three such decisions: one at each decision point.

However, the business process dealing with exceptions to the straight-through process usually requires not just the principal decision value but also some explanation of the decision to provide guidance to people dealing with the case and to provide an audit trail. A simple and convenient way of providing an explanation is in the form of a list of reasons. These reasons are often used to manage the review activity; the reviewer must make a judgment on each referral reason listed and must mark every one "accept" for the case to proceed. Note that the review activity can then be managed by the BPMS, using the referral information provided by the decision service; the case does not need to return to the decision service for the BRMS to evaluate the results of the review.

You can guarantee the completeness of the rule set by adopting a default decision value and using the rules only to describe exceptions to this decision. Typically the default decision is "accept" or "continue," and the rules indicate when a case should be referred or declined. This approach seems counterintuitive to some who prefer to think of a default decision of "decline" and a set of conditions for the case being accepted. However, a moment's thought will make clear why this is not a good approach.

Let's say there are 20 conditions for eligibility, starting with:

- Age ≥ 18
- Residency = local
- Not bankrupt

These cannot be framed as separate rules, because it is not true that an applicant over 18 should always be accepted, nor that a local resident should always be accepted. A rule set to accept the case would have to consist of a single rule with 20 conditions:

- IF age ≥ 18 and residency = local and not bankrupt and [17 more conditions] THEN route = "accept."

This is very unwieldy for maintenance and if the conditions are not met the rule simply fails to fire; you get no information as to the reasons for nonacceptance. The alternative approach, adopting accept as the default decision, gives you:

- IF age <18 THEN route = "decline."
- IF residency ≠ local THEN route = "decline."
- IF bankrupt THEN route = "decline."
- and 17 more rules

This provides 20 independent rules that can be conveniently exposed for editing through a knowledge maintenance interface.

Usually, there will be rules for two or more category values in the rule set (for example, refer and decline). As I explained in Chapter 3, there should be a defined set of priorities among these categories, not among the rules themselves, that should be order-independent. Each rule can therefore be thought of as proposing a category, and the final result should be the highest priority category proposed by any rule that fires.

To provide an audit trail, you can associate a reason with each rule, to be recorded when the rule fires, possibly together with other information such as:

- For a referral: the review team to which the case should be referred
- For a decline: whether the decline may later be overridden

The decision service should return the overall result, plus a list of all the rules that fired.

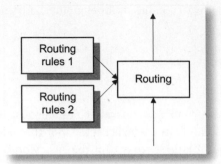

FIGURE 6.1   DRD Component for Category with Reasons Pattern

Pattern

The Category with Reasons pattern is shown in Figures 6.1 and 6.2.

DRD:
- A single decision node with one or more knowledge nodes, each holding a single rule set for one area of rules, as shown in Figure 6.1. The results of the decision are a category and a list of reasons.

Knowledge:
- A set of decision values, one of which is designated as the default category, and an order of priorities for conflict resolution (as discussed in Chapter 2).
- One or more rule sets, each describing exceptions to the default decision, containing rules in the form "IF <conditions> THEN propose (<category>, <reason>)." All rules (apart from abstractions) should use the same proposal function: this allows multiple rule sets to be combined in a single decision.

Object model:
- A decision object with a single category property and list of reasons.
- A Reason object recording the category proposed by a single rule, the associated reason, and any other properties as necessary.

    Figure 6.2 shows an example of the object model for an application routing decision where the category is a route. Note that the Routing object could be reused for other similar decisions.

Decision infrastructure:
- A single task in the decision flow, which initializes the decision category to the default value, then applies all the rule sets in the associated knowledge areas.

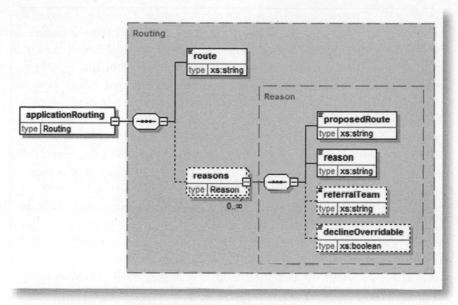

FIGURE 6.2   Object Model for Category with Reasons Pattern

- A proposal function to implement the action of the rules, which adds a reason to the list of reasons and updates the decision category if the proposed category is higher priority than the current category.

Rules with Recorded Exceptions

Usage

As an analyst, you know a job is about to get interesting when you try to confirm with the subject matter expert that a set of business rules completely defines an organization's policy and the response is, "Yes, except . . ."

Exceptions can be hard to model, because they are often very specific and may have special implications for the business process. For example, let's say we have a general policy rule that says a charge of a certain type (x) is not eligible for payment unless it has been authorized in a certain way (y). This might be stated something like: "IF charge type = x and not (authorization type = y) THEN payment = ineligible." Now imagine we have one particular supplier (z) who, for historical reasons, has a contractual dispensation and does not need to obtain this authorization. We could represent this rule, with its exception, as "IF charge type = x and not (authorization type = y) and not (supplier = z) THEN payment = ineligible." Job done.

Except . . . there are problems with this approach. First, there might be a number of such exceptions, perhaps many. If all these exceptions are added as "and not" conditions, our nice, simple, general business rule becomes a bramble bush. Second, these detailed operational exceptions need to be managed by different staff and on a different timescale from the underlying strategic business policies, which remain fairly static. These problems can be addressed by separating the general rule from the exceptions. The policy rule becomes: "IF charge type = x and not (authorization type = y) and not (payment authorization exception) THEN payment = ineligible." The exceptions can then form a separate set of independent rules, including our original "IF supplier = z THEN payment authorization exception."

But we are not quite finished. What happens when supplier z submits an invoice without authorization, and the decision service quite correctly allows it to be paid? If the payment authorization rule is well-known throughout the organization, isn't there a significant chance that someone will intercept the payment and assume the computer made a mistake? When a business policy is widely known, we may need the *exception* to be recorded against the case as an explanation for the deviation from policy. We therefore need the exception rules to contribute to the list of reasons returned by the policy decision. When a policy applies, we should see in the list either a reason for upholding the policy or a reason for waiving it.

Pattern

The pattern for Rules with Recorded Exceptions is an extension of the pattern for Category with Reasons. It is shown in Figures 6.3 and 6.4.

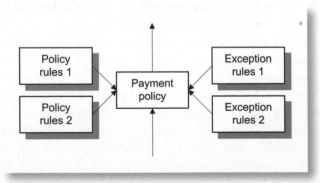

FIGURE 6.3 DRD Component for Rules with Recorded Exceptions Pattern

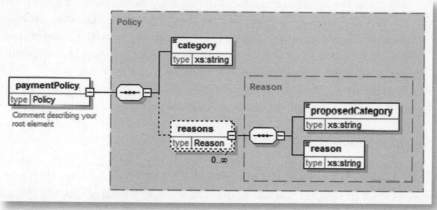

FIGURE 6.4 Object Model for Rules with Recorded Exceptions Pattern

DRD:
- A single decision node with separate knowledge nodes for each area of policy rules and exception rules, as shown in Figure 6.3. The results of the decision are a category and a list of reasons.

Knowledge:
- A set of decision values, one of which is designated as the default category and an order of priorities for conflict resolution (as discussed in Chapter 2), typically decline > refer > accept.
- One or more policy rule sets, containing rules in the form "IF <conditions> and not <exceptions> THEN propose (<category>, <reason>)."
- One or more exception rule sets, containing rules in the form "IF <conditions> THEN <exception>; propose (<default category>, <reason>)."

Object model:
- A decision object with a single category property and list of reasons.
- A Reason object recording the category proposed by a single rule, the associated reason, and any other properties as necessary.

    The object model for Rules with Recorded Exceptions will be the same as that for Category with Reasons (see Figure 6.4). The example we described here does not require the additional fields for routing.

Decision infrastructure:
- A single task in the decision flow, which initializes the decision category to the default value, then applies all the rule sets in the associated knowledge areas.

- A proposal function to implement the action of both policy and exception rules, which adds a reason to the list of reasons and updates the decision category if the proposed category is higher priority than the current category. When called by an exception rule the category proposed is the default, so the decision category will not be updated.
- A chaining mechanism to evaluate the exception rules as required by the policy rules. How exactly this works will depend on your BRMS.

Segmented Score Model

Usage

As described in Chapter 3, a scorecard is an analytic model consisting of a set of rules for calculating a predictive score. However, a single scorecard is rarely used on its own; the model may be segmented into multiple scorecards, and it may be protected by exclusion rules that identify cases that are not covered by the model. Normally, a scoring decision consists of three stages:

1. Using a set of rules, the case is either excluded from scoring or placed into a segment for scoring. The segment selected determines which scorecard will be used.
2. A set of characteristics specific to the score model to be used is derived by combining various input data using calculations or logical expressions. For example, a "family type" characteristic might be derived from marital status and number of dependents.
3. The selected scorecard is applied, placing each of its characteristics into a bin (a range of values) that determines a partial score (its contribution to the score), and adding all these partial scores together.

These three stages are logically part of the same scoring decision, so it is useful to be able to represent them as such in the DRD and implement them using a single task in the decision flow.

Pattern

The segmented score model pattern is shown in Figures 6.5 and 6.6.

DRD:
- A single decision node with multiple knowledge nodes:
  - One knowledge node for the segmentation rules
  - One knowledge node for each score model

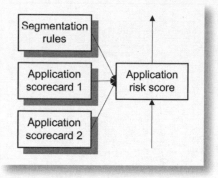

FIGURE 6.5 DRD Component for Segmented Score Model Pattern

The results of the decision are a segment, a score, and the list of partial results. Figure 6.5 shows the DRD for a score model with two segments.

Knowledge:
- A set of segmentation rules, placing the case into one of the segments, or labeling it as excluded.
- A score model for each segment, including the characteristic derivations and scoring rules.

Object model:
- A ScoreModelResults object with a segment property, a list of characteristics, and the final score.
- A Characteristic object recording the name, allocated bin, and partial score for each characteristic.

Figure 6.6 shows a ScoreModelResults object used to return the results from the application risk score decision. This object could be reused by other score model decisions.

Decision infrastructure:
- A single task in the decision flow, which applies the segmentation rules to determine the segment, then either applies the appropriate scorecard to calculate the score, or (if the segment is excluded) provides some symbolic value (such as zero).

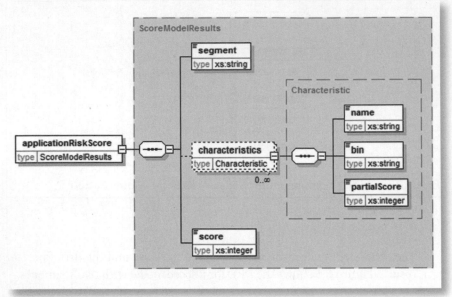

FIGURE 6.6 Object Model for Segmented Score Model Pattern

Champion-Challenger

Usage

Most of the business knowledge expressed in decision services is not correct in any absolute sense, but only current best practice. It must be frequently updated, by expressing new business policies in new analytic models, rule sets, and so on. However, it would be a brave organization that simply switched over to these new policies without testing them first. *Champion-challenger* is a commonly used approach to test the effectiveness of business policy, using the feedback cycle shown in Figure 3.3, without exposing the organization to excessive risk.

At any time, there may be several versions of the business knowledge determining a decision: a champion and a number of challengers. Each of these is known as a "strategy." The champion strategy represents the current best practice; the challenger strategies represent alternative policies to be tested. Each case is randomly allocated to a strategy for decision-making. Most cases will be allocated to the champion, but a small percentage will be allocated to the challengers. The success of the challengers can then be compared with that of the champion by collecting feedback from the process and from the subsequent behavior of the customer over time. If any of the challenger strategies are shown to be more successful than the champion, the champion is replaced by that challenger, and the cycle begins again.

Here are two pieces of advice when using champion-challenger:

1. The policies associated with each strategy should be different versions of *complete knowledge areas*; for example, a whole rule set, table, or model. Do not attempt to apply champion-challenger to individual rules or characteristics: it makes analysis of the results very difficult.
2. Allocate cases to strategies randomly, using a pseudorandom number. For example, pick a random integer between 0 and 99, and use a table like Table 6.1 to assign cases to strategies based on this number (the strategy code). Do not just count sequentially and allocate every nth case to a challenger; this might seem preferable but can lead to contamination of the samples due to nonrandom effects in the business process (for example, batching of cases in work queues). In Table 6.1, 90 percent of cases are allocated to the champion strategy, 5 percent to challenger 1, and 5 percent to challenger 2.

Note that it is important that whatever strategy is allocated to a customer, this same strategy is used at every decision point throughout the business process. The strategy code is therefore usually chosen by the BPMS and passed into each decision service.

Pattern

The champion-challenger pattern is shown in Figures 6.7 and 6.8. The pattern is demonstrated using the Application Risk Grade decision in Table 6.1, but could be used for any decision.

DRD:
- A single decision node with multiple knowledge nodes:
  - One knowledge node for the strategy table
  - One knowledge node for each strategy

TABLE 6.1   Champion-Challenger Strategy Table

Decision	Strategy Code	Strategy
Application Risk Grade	0–89	Champion
Application Risk Grade	90–94	Challenger 1
Application Risk Grade	94–99	Challenger 2

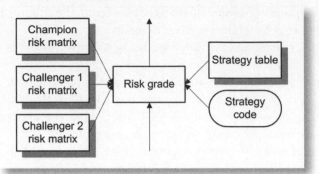

FIGURE 6.7   DRD Component for Champion-Challenger Pattern

The decision results should include the segment used in order to support subsequent analysis. Figure 6.7 shows the DRD for a risk grade decision using three versions of a risk matrix: a champion and two challengers.

Knowledge:
- A strategy table, using the strategy code to determine the strategy. This table might be used for multiple decisions.
- A complete version of the knowledge required by the decision for each strategy.

Object model:
- The normal results for the decision, extended with a strategy property, identifying the strategy used.
  Figure 6.8 shows a RiskGrade object used to return the results from the application risk grade decision.

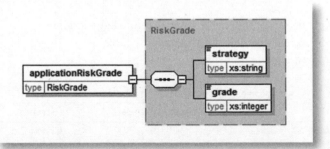

FIGURE 6.8   Object Model for Champion-Challenger Pattern

Decision infrastructure:
- A single task in the decision flow, which applies the strategy table to determine the strategy, then applies the appropriate knowledge area (the appropriate risk matrix in the example shown in Figure 6.7).

 ## COLLABORATIVE DECISION-MAKING

This book has deliberately focused on the use of decision services to automate operational decisions. But it is not always possible or desirable to hand over all responsibility for business decisions to a decision service; sometimes a BRMS is required to assist or collaborate with the user in decision-making. There are two fundamentally different approaches to collaborative decision-making: referrals, and the more subtle area of decision support.

Referrals

The principle behind referrals is the idea that cases can be partitioned according to whether they can be handled automatically, or whether they must be dealt with by a person. If the logic for this partitioning can be expressed in clear rules, an efficient approach for automation is for the partitioning itself to be carried out by a decision service. It is then possible to have a fully automatic straight-through process, using human contact only for exceptions.

Two types of referrals have already been discussed extensively in Chapters 2 and 5: levels of authority and triage.

Levels of Authority

The simplest type of referral decision is achieved by defining a level of authority for the decision service and passing across for human decision any cases above this level. Often this approach is extended to include several approval levels, determining which person the case should be referred to, as shown in Figure 2.3. Some business logic is needed to determine the measure to be compared to approval level; depending on the business domain this might be the potential value of sale, the potential risk of the case, or the amount to be underwritten. This value can be compared with thresholds in an approval table, as shown in Table 2.2. Measures can also be combined, either by using a weighted function to produce an overall measure or by defining referral rules referring to multiple measures in their conditions.

Triage

One simple and commonly used method for referrals is triage, usually applied in circumstances considerably less grim than the original application of this technique: deciding whether to provide medical treatment to a casualty on the battlefield. Cases are partitioned into three sets: those with a clear positive decision, those with a clear negative decision, and marginal cases that must be referred for human review. This is the accept/refer/decline approach to routing decisions described in Chapters 2 and 5.

Triage is usually implemented using two sets of rules: decline rules (defining the partition of cases that can clearly be rejected) and refer rules (defining the partition of the remaining cases that need to go for review). Cases that are not subject to any decline or refer rules are accepted using straight-through processing. Note that under this system there is no attempt to define business rules that provide a clear, universal definition of which cases should be accepted. The boundary of this set lies somewhere in the refer partition.

Under triage, the decision service and the user are ultimately responsible for different cases. The decision service is responsible for the accept/decline decision on clear cases and for referring marginal cases to the user. The user is responsible for the accept/decline decision on the referred cases.

Decision Support

An alternative approach is to allow collaboration between the decision service and the user on each case, rather than have responsibility for a whole case fall to either the decision service or the user. This is sometimes called decision support: the assumption being that the decision service supports the user (although, as we shall see, it is not always that simple). There is a spectrum of techniques available for decision support, depending on the respective roles of the user and the decision service, that is, how responsibility for the decision is allocated between the two collaborating decision makers. The three techniques described in this chapter are:

1. The decision service advises the user.
2. The decision service constrains the user.
3. The user constrains the decision service.

These are listed in order of increasing responsibility for the decision service.

Whichever technique is used, it is of vital importance that the roles of the user and the decision service are clearly defined from the outset. Human-computer interaction is a prime opportunity for really messy design. Whatever role it is allocated in the interaction, the contribution of the decision service can always be framed in terms of decisions and analyzed using DRA.

Decision Service Advises the User

Using this approach, the user has full flexibility and authority in his or her decision-making, but the decision service offers advice or suggestions (see Figure 6.9).

Be warned: This is deceptively difficult to do well if you approach the problem the wrong way, that is, if you see the purpose of the decision service being to choose a piece of advisory text to display to the user. Deciding what advice to give in a certain situation is hard, because it depends not only on the characteristics of the case but also on the needs of the users and how they view the case, which is information not readily available to the decision service. If you are not careful you end up with thousands of rules responding

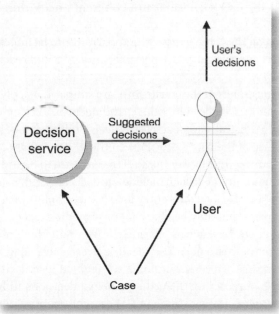

FIGURE 6.9   Decision Service Advises the User

to very specific scenarios, and no easy way to structure or maintain them. The key to applying this technique effectively is to remember that the decision service is giving the user advice on what decision is to be made, so a much easier approach is simply for the decision service to make the decision, then suggest and explain it.

This use of a decision service is then essentially identical to its use in automation, except in the way the results are used in the business process. Instead of being returned to the BPMS to influence the process, the decision service results are only displayed to the user. The user then makes his own decisions, and it is these that are applied in the process. However, the decision service may be broader in scope than for automation, for example, it may be required to list all the possible solutions rather than choose the best. There may also be more emphasis on explanation than in automation: for example, a list of reasons for a few selected decisions may not be sufficient; it may be necessary to provide a full trace of the decision logic.

Decision Service Constrains the User

In this technique, the user has responsibility for decision-making on the case, but is constrained by the decision service, which is responsible for ensuring that the user's decisions are coherent and within legal or policy constraints.

Depending on the complexity of the constraints to be imposed on the user, two quite different approaches are possible: proactive and reactive.

1. *Proactive constraints.* If the constraints are simple and apply independently to individual user decision values, the decision service can determine appropriate constraints for each of the decisions to be made by user, and the conformance of the user's decisions to those constraints can be enforced through the user interface or BPMS. This is shown in Figure 6.10. Common applications for this approach include the decision service setting the range of values allowable for a data entry field (for example, upper and lower limits on the price that may be charged) or providing a set of possible values for a drop-down list (such as offering the user only those products that are available to the customer). The "decline overridable" flag in Figure 6.2 is also an example of a constraint on a subsequent user decision.

   For the purposes of DRA, the principal decisions to be taken by the decision service are the values of these constraints, not the decisions subsequently taken by the user.

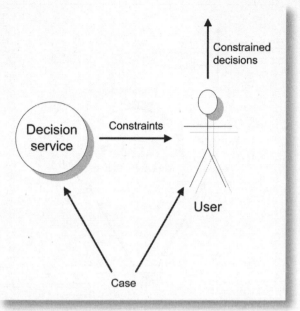

FIGURE 6.10 Decision Service Constrains the User—Proactive Constraints

2. *Reactive constraints.* If we wish to impose complex constraints addressing the relationships between user decisions, for example to ensure that a set of decisions is consistent, we must use the opposite approach. The user proposes some decisions, then the decision service is called to check that the decisions conform to the constraints. This is shown in Figure 6.11. Here the user's proposals are the input data for the decision service; the service makes a set of decisions on whether those proposals conform to the constraints and bounces them back to the user if they do not, with explanations of what is wrong. The user adjusts his or her proposed decisions until they are approved by the decision service.

User Constrains the Decision Service

Using this final technique for collaboration, all decision-making is carried out by the decision service but constrained by the user. The user's constraints are often described as "overrides." This is shown in Figure 6.12. This technique is used when there is a complex structure of interrelated decisions, and you want users to be able to override individual components within that structure but want the decision service to ensure that the overall structure of decisions is

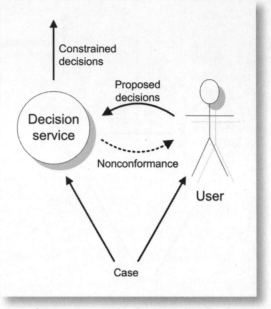

FIGURE 6.11   Decision Service Constrains the User—Reactive Constraints

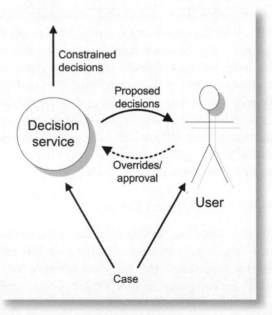

FIGURE 6.12   User Constrains the Decision Service

correct and consistent. An important principle to be remembered here is that you never override rules; you only override decisions.

A good example would be a system for insurance claims adjudication, where the claim consists of many component charges, and there are complex rules governing the allowable combinations of charges and how they are added up to provide the final total amount payable. The decision service should provide an initial assessment of the claim, with values for all the component items, intermediate values, and a total. The adjudicator should then be able to exercise discretion by overriding one or more component amounts; the decision service would then recalculate the total, using the adjudicator's overrides in preference to its own decisions, wherever they have been provided.

The simplest approach is to present the user with the whole structure of decisions from the decision service and allow them to override any decision value. The decision service can then be called again, providing the original case data plus the overrides, which should be represented using exactly the same object model as used to output the decisions. As the decision service evaluates each of its decisions, it should first check to see whether that decision value has already been provided by the user as an override. If an override has been provided, the decision service simply copies it into the equivalent position in its output; if not, it continues to evaluate the decision in the normal way.

This interaction between user and decision service can be repeated, with the user overriding different decisions and observing the effect on the overall result, until they are satisfied with the result and approve it. This is the most complex of the techniques for decision support but results in a system that uses the best features of the human user and the decision service and is truly collaborative.

Conclusion

I N THESE SIX CHAPTERS we have traveled down through the higher levels of a knowledge automation project, from the very top—the motivating business strategy—down to the techniques used to implement business knowledge in decision services. This was our journey:

- Chapter 1 began with the fundamental truth that business knowledge has a measurable value and showed that this value can be realized as *decision yield* by using the techniques of *decision management* to automate operational business decision-making.

- Chapter 2 explained that such decision-making can be modeled as a set of *decision points* in the business process, and automated by *decision services* that encapsulate the business knowledge required to make those decisions. These services are exposed by a business rules management system (BRMS) and called by the business process management system (BPMS). Using decision services efficiently may involve some process redesign to rationalize the decision points; a template automated originations business process was described as an example.

- Chapter 3 presented the most important technologies used to encapsulate knowledge in decision services—*business rules* (including decision tables and decision trees), *algorithms*, and *predictive analytics* (including induction, scorecards, and neural nets)—and discussed their relative strengths and weaknesses. It presented the overall architecture used for automating decisions and showed that the four main components (BPMS, BRMS, predictive analytic modeling, and data warehousing) support the decision management cycle.

- Chapter 4 introduced *Decision Requirements Analysis* (DRA), explained its intent, and presented its principles. It proposed the simple workshop technique DRAW, which decomposes decision-making into a structure that can be represented graphically in a *Decision Requirements Diagram* (DRD).

The DRD shows the relationships between *decisions*, *knowledge areas*, and *data areas*, and allows the scope of a project to be defined in these terms.

▪ Chapter 5 showed how the structure of the DRD can be used to organize all aspects of a *knowledge automation project*: scoping, estimation, planning, knowledge discovery, design, development, configuration, and testing. It showed that the modularization of decision-making through DRA allowed the creation of a *knowledge production line* for efficient delivery.

▪ Chapter 6 finished with some concrete examples of *common decision patterns* and discussed how to achieve *collaborative decision-making* involving interaction between decision services and business users.

This brings us to the limit of the detail that can be discussed in this book, in which I have tried to remain product-neutral throughout. To proceed any further would involve discussing technical issues specific to individual BRMS products, design tools, or architectural environments. For further detail you should consult product reviews and contact suppliers.

Rather than present anything you could properly call a theory, I have tried to convey a way of seeing things, a way of approaching projects, and a vocabulary. The principles of DRA are very simple—almost embarrassingly simple—but, I believe, no less valuable for that. The key concept is that decision-making has a *structure* that can be represented graphically, and that if you can capture that structure it can be used to support all the work in a knowledge automation project. The benefits are better communication, clearer scope, more efficient delivery, and reduced risk.

Even if you do not adopt DRA completely, just using the vocabulary will be a boon: distinguishing carefully between decision points, decision services, decisions, knowledge areas, rules, algorithms, and models. Too often the word "rules" is used to cover all of these, and the result is confusion.

So in summary, here are my 10 tips (I hesitate to call them commandments) for successful knowledge automation:

1. Justify your potential knowledge automation projects in terms of their decision yield.
2. Do not automate your existing process: redesign your process for automation.
3. Clearly identify decision points in the business process where only automated decision-making will be carried out.
4. Even when using services for decision support, analyze them in terms of decision-making.

5. Define the decision-making to be automated using DRAW and use the decision structure exposed in the DRD to inform all subsequent activities.

6. Define the scope of automation and the functionality of individual decision services by drawing boundaries around subgraphs of the DRD.

7. Construct an iterative project plan by partitioning the DRD into increments of functionality and identifying the dependencies between the increments.

8. Guide knowledge discovery by constraining it to the knowledge areas to be automated in each increment.

9. Use the DRD to suggest a design for the decision flow and object model and a reusable implementation type for each decision

10. Create a knowledge production line with traceability of all deliverables to the original requirements.

I sincerely hope this approach will help you and wish you every success with your knowledge automation projects.

Glossary

A

algorithm   A procedure for determining some result from a set of input data, expressed as a sequence of computational steps, and usually implemented in software as a function.

automation scoping document   A document containing the results of DRAW, defining the scope of the decision-making to be automated in a process automation project.

B

back-propagation   A method for adjusting the weightings on the connections in a neural network to minimize the error in the network's prediction.

backward chaining   A strategy for reasoning in rule-based systems, in which the DRE starts with a hypothesis to be proven, and evaluates only those rules that are necessary to establish that result. Also known as goal-directed reasoning.

business intelligence (BI)   A set of technologies for aggregating, analyzing, filtering, and presenting data to assist executives in their decision-making without actually making their decisions for them.

business process management (BPM)   The professional discipline concerned with designing and implementing business processes to maximize their value to the organization.

business process management system (BPMS)   A computer system that manages a business process by executing a sequence of activities defined in a business process model.

business process model   A flow diagram specifying the constituent activities of a process and showing how these activities are dependent on one another.

Business Process Modeling Notation (BPMN)   A standard for representing business process models in such a way that they can be directly executed by a BPMS.

business rule   An "atom" of business knowledge, expressed in the form IF <conditions> THEN <conclusion>.

business rule engine (BRE)   The component of a BRMS that executes business knowledge, including business rules. Also known as the inference engine.

business rules management system (BRMS)   A software environment for building decision-making systems, including a repository for business knowledge, a business rules engine, a development environment, facilities for creating knowledge maintenance interfaces, and tools for deploying decision services.

C

champion-challenger   A technique for testing the effectiveness of new business policies without exposing the organization to excessive risk, by using the current champion strategy for the majority of cases, and alternative challenger strategies for a randomly selected minority, and comparing their effectiveness statistically.

completeness   The property of a rule set where the decision result is defined for all possible combinations of input data values.

consistency   The property of a rule set where either only one rule fires for any case, or, if multiple rules fire, there is some way of determining the correct result.

D

data-directed reasoning   See forward chaining.

decision   The determination of a set of results from a set of data using business knowledge.

decision management (DM)   The use of machine learning and automated decision-making to improve the profitability of business decisions. Also known as enterprise decision management.

decision point   A point in a business process where one or more decisions are required to be made by a decision service.

Decision Process Specification   A business process modeling technique developed by Paul Konnersman, in which decisions are modeled as activities involving people in five roles: decision manager, consultee, approver, inspector, and informee.

Decision Requirements Analysis (DRA)   A technique for decomposing decision-making by defining what information is required for each decision: areas of business knowledge, areas of data, and the results of other decisions. The results can be presented as a DRD.

Decision Requirements Analysis Workshop (DRAW)   A structured workshop technique for defining the decision-making requirements for a set of decision services and documenting them using DRDs.

Decision Requirements Diagram (DRD)   A network diagram showing the structure of a domain of decision-making as a network of decisions and subdecisions, with their supporting areas of business knowledge and data.

decision service   A service that takes a set of data describing a case and returns one or more decisions on the case by applying some encapsulated business knowledge.

decision table   A rule metaphor that presents a rule set as a table with a column for each property used in the conditions and a column for each property set in the conclusions. Each row in the table represents a business rule.

decision tree   A rule metaphor that presents a rule set as a tree that classifies a case. Each possible path through the tree represents a business rule; each node in the tree is a condition, and the terminal nodes are the possible classifications.

decision yield   A method for predicting and measuring return on investment on decision management projects, developed by FICO, which evaluates decision-making performance on five dimensions: precision, cost, speed, agility, and consistency.

E

encapsulation   The approach adopted in SOA where the internal logic of a service is hidden from consumers of the service, who only see the results.

enterprise decision management (EDM)   See decision management.

F

fact model   See object model.

Fair Isaac Rational Unified Process (FIRUP)   The RUP-based project management methodology used by FICO.

forward chaining   A strategy for reasoning in rule-based systems, in which the BRE starts with the data provided and establishes all the results that can be inferred from those data. Also known as data-directed reasoning.

G

goal-directed reasoning   See backward chaining.

I

increment   The additional functionality delivered by one iteration of a project run under iterative project management (for example, RUP).

inductive logic programming (ILP)   A technique of machine learning, which uses logical induction and generalization to generate a set of rules that is consistent with a provided set of facts.

induction   A form of reasoning that makes generalizations from particular observations in order to arrive at a set of general rules. Induction can be used to generate rules and decision trees automatically from case data.

inference   The use of business rules to derive a conclusion from a set of data.

inference engine   See business rules engine.

inheritance   The principle in object models that all the properties of an object are also properties of any objects that are types, subclasses, or instances of it. For example, Mimi (my cat) has all the properties of a cat, and a cat has all the properties of a mammal.

integration testing   The task of proving that the various components of a software solution work together and interface with each other properly.

iteration   A subdivision of a project run under iterative project management (for example, RUP) that results in the delivery of an increment of functionality.

iterative project management (IPM)   An approach to project management in which the project is broken into a series of mini-projects or iterations. Each iteration addresses all the phases of the software life cycle—requirements, design, construction, and test—to implement an increment of functionality.

K

knowledge automation   The use of decision management, business process management systems and service-oriented architecture to automate decision-making in business processes.

knowledge-based system   A system that can model business knowledge (for example, as business rules) and deploy it in a decision service.

knowledge discovery   The collection of business knowledge from domain experts and its codification in an executable form (for example, business rules or algorithms). Also known as rule discovery.

M

machine learning   A set of technologies for creating knowledge, in the form of predictive models, from data.

multilayer perceptron (MLP)   A commonly used form of neural network, consisting of a layer of input nodes, a number of hidden layers, and an output layer.

mutually exclusive   The property of a set of rules in which only one rule fires for any set of input data.

N

neural network   A form of machine learning achieved by simulating a network of simplified nerve cells. Learning is achieved through changes in the weightings of the connections between the cells.

O

Object Management Group (OMG)   A standards institution responsible for BPMN and SBVR.

object model   A structured vocabulary defining the entities to be described in a domain of knowledge and their relationships to one another. Also known as fact model and ontology.

ontology   See object model.

outside-In   An approach to process design that starts with the desired customer journey and provides business processes as required to serve the customer.

P

predictive analytics   A field of techniques for analyzing historical data recording what actually happened in a representative set of cases and using the analysis to create models that will predict objectively what will happen in similar cases in the future.

predictive model   A mathematical model created using a predictive analytical technique, which predicts a set of outcomes given a set of data.

pseudocode   An informal but structured language that approximates a nonspecific programming language, used for specifying algorithms.

R

Rational Unified Process (RUP)   An iterative project management methodology, which divides projects into four phases: inception, elaboration, construction, and transition.

Rete   An algorithm that optimizes the inference strategy of business rule engines.

rule discovery   See knowledge discovery.

rule metaphor   A way of representing a rule set to make it more easily understood by the business user, for example, as a decision table or decision tree.

rule set   A set of business rules that together make a single decision.

S

scorecard   A predictive model that predicts the likelihood of a particular event by summing a number of weighted characteristics to produce a numerical score. Used for application scoring, behavior scoring, and credit scoring. Also known as score model.

segmentation   A technique for improving the predictiveness of models by partitioning the population of cases into segments and building a separate model for each segment. The segmentation is often represented as a decision tree.

service-oriented architecture (SOA)   The provision of software functionality as loosely coupled, reusable services that encapsulate their internal logic to hide it from the consumers.

U

unit testing   The task of proving that a single component behaves as intended, before it is delivered for integration and user testing.

user testing   The task of demonstrating to the users' satisfaction that the delivered system meets all their requirements.

W

waterfall approach   An approach to project management in which each phase of the software lifecycle—requirements, design, construction, and test—is completed before moving on to the next.

Suggested Reading

Books and Papers

Davenport, T. A., J. G. Harris, and R. Morison. *Analytics at Work: Smarter Decisions, Better Results*. Boston: Harvard Business School, 2010.

Debevoise, T. *Business Process Management with a Business Rules Approach: Implementing the Service Oriented Architecture*. Lexington, VA: Tipping Point Solutions, 2007.

Debevoise, T. and R. Geneva. *The Microguide to Process Modeling in BPMN: How to Build Great Process, Rule, and Event Models*. Lexington, VA: Tipping Point Solutions.

Fausett, L. *Fundamentals of Neural Networks: Architectures, Algorithms and Applications*. Upper Saddle River, NJ: Prentice-Hall, 1994.

Gilovich, T., D. W. Griffin, and D. Kahneman. *Heuristics and Biases: The Psychology of Intuitive Judgment*. New York: Cambridge University Press, 2002.

Graham, I. *Business Rules Management and Service Oriented Architecture: A Pattern Language*. Chichester, UK: John Wiley & Sons, 2006.

Harmon, P. *Business Process Change: A Guide for Business Managers and BPM and Six Sigma Professionals*, 2nd edition. Burlington, MA: Morgan Kaufmann Publishers, 2007.

Konnersman, P. M. *Decision Process Specification: A Process for Defining Professional and Managerial Work Processes*. Portland International Conference on Management of Engineering and Technology, July 27–31, 1997, Portland, Oregon.

Kruchten, P. *The Rational Unified Process: An Introduction*, 3rd ed. Boston: Addison-Wesley, 2003.

Morgan, T. *Business Rules and Information Systems: Aligning IT with Business Goals*. Boston: Addison-Wesley, 2002.

Rational, *Rational Unified Process: Best Practices for Software Development Teams*. Rational Software White Paper TP026B, rev. 11/01, 2001.

Rosenberger, L. E., and J. Nash. *The Deciding Factor: The Power of Analytics to Make Every Decision a Winner*. San Francisco: Jossey-Bass, 2009.

Ross, R. G. *Principles of Business Rule Approach*. Boston: Addison-Wesley, 2003.

Ross, R. G. *Business Rule Concepts: Getting to the Point of Knowledge*. Houston: Business Rule Solutions, LLC, 2009.

Ross, R. G. and G. S. W. Lam. *Building Business Solutions: Business Analysis with Business Rules*. International Institute of Business Analysis handbook. Houston: Business Rule Solutions, LLC, 2011.

Taylor, J. *Smart (Enough) Systems: How to Deliver Competitive Advantage by Automating Hidden Decisions*. Boston: Pearson Education Inc., 2007.

Taylor, J. *Decision Management Systems: A Practical Guide to Using Business Rules and Predictive Analytics*. IBM Press, 2011.

Von Halle, B., L. Goldberg, and J. Zachman, *Business Rule Revolution: Running Business the Right Way*. Silicon Valley: Happy About, 2006.

Von Halle, B. *Business Rules Applied: Building Better Systems Using the Business Rule Approach*. New York: John Wiley & Sons,2001.

Von Halle, B. and L. Goldberg,. *The Decision Model: A Business Logic Framework Linking Business and Technology*. Boca Raton, FL: Auerbach Publications, 2010.

Websites and Blogs

The Business Rules Manifesto: The Principles of Rule Independence. (Ed. Ronald Ross). www.businessrulesgroup.org/brmanifesto.htm.

BPM Focus. http://www.waria.com

Business Process Management Initiative. http://www.bpmi.org

Business Process Trends. http://www.bptrends.com

Business Rules Community. http://www.brcommunity.com

Business Rules Group. http://www.businessrulesgroup.org

Complex Event Processing (blog). (Ed. Paul Vincent). http://tibcoblogs.com/cep.

Decision Management (blog). (ed. James Taylor). http://www.ebizq.net/blogs/decision_management

Everything Decision Management, Technically Speaking (blog). (Ed. Carole-Ann Matignon and Carlos Serrano-Morales). http://techondec.wordpress.com.

FICO Decision Management (blog). http://dmblog.fico.com.

FICO Decision Management Community. http://exchange.fico.com/dmc

International Institute for Analytics. http://iianalytics.com.

Wanderings of the Mind: JavaRules (blog). (Ed. James Owen). http://javarules .blogspot.com.

Jim Sinur (blog). http://blogs.gartner.com/jim_sinur.

JT on EDM (blog). (Ed. James Taylor). http://jtonedm.com.

Object Management Group. http://www.omg.org

Primatek Consulting (blog). (Ed. Eric Charpentier). http://www.primatek.ca/ blog.

Process Modeling 2.0 (blog). (Ed. Tom Debevoise). www.tomdebevoise.com.

Requirements Networking Group. http://www.requirementsnetwork.com

Sparkling Logic Community. http://community.sparklinglogic.com

About the Author

Alan Fish is an authority on the use of business rules and predictive analytics for decision management. His innovations in this field include new methodologies for decision service analysis, design and development, including the technique of Decision Requirements Analysis (DRA). His background in psychology, statistics, and artificial intelligence allows him to combine human expertise, predictive analytics, and business rules in adaptive decision-making systems.

Alan has been building decision-making systems for 30 years and has been responsible for many significant projects at the forefront of current technology. He has worked in many diverse domains over this time, including defense, robotics, industrial process control, government, utilities asset management, insurance, and retail credit originations.

Alan is currently principal consultant in Decision Solutions with FICO, working in Europe, Middle East, and Africa. Previously, he was the managing director of a small consultancy specializing in applications of rule-based systems and data mining, which he ran for 12 years. Before that he was employed as a consultant in artificial intelligence and human factors by a number of international IT systems companies. He holds a BSc in psychology and a PhD in neural networks, both from the University of Manchester.

Alan lives with his wife and two young children in the house he built by the sea on his wife's croft land on the Isle of Lewis (in the Outer Hebrides, Scotland), where he keeps sheep and chickens. He also has four grown children. His major interest is music of all kinds: He sings with classical chamber choirs, *a cappella* ensembles, and a swing band; he is a guitarist and singer-songwriter; he writes modern classical compositions and jazz arrangements; he plays the saxophone very badly. He also enjoys walking, reading, cooking, and "good craic" with friends, preferably accompanied by whisky and the smell of peat smoke.

Index